Effective BUSINESS WRITING

The Everyday
Guide to Clear,
Concise and
Powerful Writing

Effective BUSINESS WRITING

The Everyday Guide to Clear, Concise and Powerful Writing

Marcia Dennis

SkillPath® Publications

Editor: Bill Cowles

Cover design: Jason Dill

Layout: Danielle Horn

ISBN: 978-1-934589-52-6

Printed in the United States of America

Table of Contents

Introduction

Do you dread writing letters, memos, e-mails, reports—any kind of business document?

Are you unsure where to start?

Is it difficult organizing your ideas?

Do you struggle with presenting your message clearly and concisely?

You'll be amazed at how much easier business writing will be—and how quickly your writing will improve—when you learn, practice and master the skills in this book.

You'll learn how to:

- Write clearly and concisely
- Get an immediate response
- Grab your reader's attention
- Overcome writer's block
- Organize your ideas and write your first draft faster
- Develop your own style
- Use the latest formatting techniques to improve readability
- Profit from editing and proofreading techniques the pros use
- Write effective business reports and proposals
- And much more

Ready to get started? Read on!

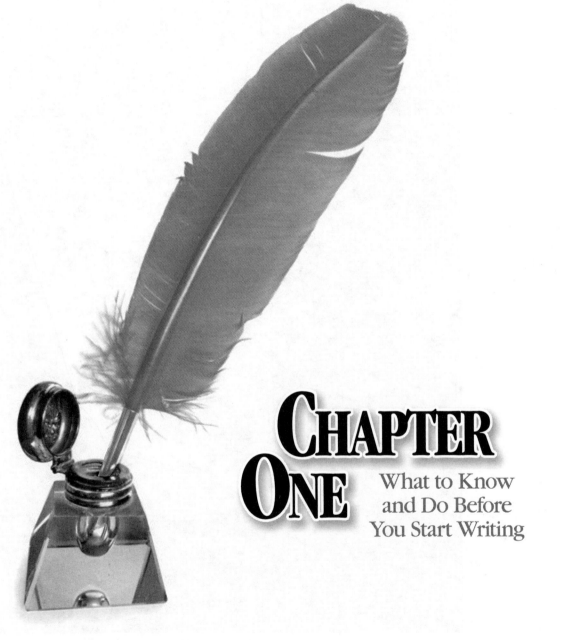

CHAPTER ONE

What to Know
and Do Before
You Start Writing

You've probably heard the saying that writing is 10% inspiration and 90% perspiration and that good writers start with a burst of energy. Wrong. One of the biggest challenges even good writers face is getting started.

Follow the Golden Rule of Business Writing

Are you one of those people who dive into a writing project without much thought? Do you feel you have to get something down on paper as soon as you can? Do you find you often have to go back and redo what you've written? Do you believe that pausing to think through what you want to say and how you want to say it is a gigantic waste of your time?

The Golden Rule of effective business writing: Take time to plan

You may be thinking at this moment: *I don't have time to plan. I need to get this out now.* The fact is, planning what to write saves you time. That's because once you plan, you have uppermost in your mind your purpose in writing, who your audience is, what action you want to stimulate, what tone is appropriate, the points you need to make to convey your message and the order in which you need to make them. It's all there.

The failure to plan your writing can be expensive. Writing a poorly executed letter, memo, e-mail or report can cost you:

- Hours of your valuable time

- Hard dollars, if your writing drives customers away

- Your career, if your boss realizes he or she can't count on you

- The respect of your staff, if they don't get what you're trying to say

- Your reputation, if your colleagues come to expect lousy writing from you

How do you approach writing? Do you sit down, write everything you can think of on the subject and mail or e-mail it—all in a few minutes or less? Most people approach writing this way. The problem with this approach is that few people are so gifted at writing that they can get it right the first time. As a result, documents written this way are confusing and too long—and may even leave out vital information.

What if you spent a few minutes organizing your thoughts before writing anything? Though it would take a few minutes longer to do this, it's a better way to approach writing because planning will help you avoid frustration and procrastination and save time.

How About You?

Why don't you plan?

- ☐ I'm way too busy.
- ☐ It's too difficult.
- ☐ I never know what I want to say until I get into it.
- ☐ None of my colleagues do.
- ☐ No need to—I just dump everything I know into the letter or memo.
- ☐ Why? It's just a quick e-mail?
- ☐ All that thinking sounds painful.
- ☐ I don't have the self-discipline.

Take a few minutes to plan and writing will be easier—guaranteed. Read on and find out how.

Answer the Two Most Important Questions

While writing is an important task, it certainly isn't the only thing you do. And, while you want to do a good job with every piece you write, you don't want to spend all day and all night doing so. You'd like some shortcuts. Some things that will make the process go faster, more smoothly and less painfully.

No matter how complicated you may allow writing to be, it really boils down to answering two simple questions: *Why am I writing this piece? Why do my readers care?* If you take the time to think about these two questions before you even put pen to paper (or touch a keyboard), writing will be less of a chore.

Why am I writing this?

If your brain is swirling with information and you're wondering how you'll ever make sense of it all and get it down clearly on paper, it's time to go back to the basics—to the purpose of the piece. Everything you write has a purpose. If you achieve that purpose, then you've done your job well. It's that simple. The purpose of writing the piece can be found in what you want the reader to do. But you have to know that yourself before you can convey it to your audience. You may be writing to educate readers, gain their trust or dazzle them with your idea. Ask yourself another question: What exactly do I want the reader to do about it? Call me? Vote for me? Read my Web site? Order? Your answer to this question will determine your purpose.

Obvious reasons for writing ...

- Inform security managers they must enforce the new parking lot rules

- Persuade the CEO of your company to agree to meet about a new proposal

- Confirm with an employee an earlier discussion about a problem behavior and how the employee will correct it

- Ask Human Resources to write a job description for the new employee you plan to hire

And not so obvious reasons...

- You want security managers to enforce the parking lot rules to protect your company from lawsuits

- You want the CEO to agree to meet with you about a new proposal before another manager convinces him it's a waste of time

- You want your employee to agree to the performance improvement plan and sign it because it's company policy

- You want Human Resources to write the job description for the new employee because then they'll be aware of the unique requirements of the job and support your request for additional training after the employee is hired

Power Tip:

Write down your purpose in one sentence. This might be difficult but you'll be amazed at how much easier writing is when you have a clear goal to accomplish.

Why does my reader care?

Once you've defined your purpose, the next step is figuring out why your audience will care. Why will they take the time to thumb through your 40-page proposal—or read *your* e-mail when they have dozens more in their inbox? If you can answer this question, you're onto something.

How important is knowing why your reader cares? Imagine you're telling your best friend about a vacation you took—a vacation she's thinking about taking. What experiences would you describe? What details would you share? Then imagine you're telling your boss. She's on her way to a meeting and has just a few seconds to listen. It's likely the two versions you give will be noticeably different in terms of what information you share, and even your tone. That's because your friend and boss will care about what you're saying for different reasons.

Do you see how knowing why your audience cares can shape everything about your message? To find out, ask:

- What are their needs, interests and concerns?

- What do they expect to find in the document you write?

- How will they use the information?

- What is most important to them?

- What are they least likely to care about?

- Is your message a low or high priority for them?

- Do they have strong opinions about your topic? Deeply held beliefs?

- Are they likely to be friendly or hostile?

You may find in the end that you can't completely satisfy everyone's concerns. But at least you can present your position strategically, while being aware of and sensitive to those concerns.

 You Try It

Think about a writing project you will work on soon. Answer each of these questions with just one sentence:

I am writing this because _____

_____

The reader cares because_____

_____

This exercise will help you focus your writing and limit it to what is essential. Everything in the document should relate to these two important sentences.

Get a Sense of Who Your Reader Is

As you slave away at your keyboard organizing your thoughts into logical points, do you have anyone in particular in mind? You should. It's easy to forget you're not writing this for yourself. You need to be able to put yourself in your audience's shoes and write what they need or want to know. Not knowing your audience is one of the biggest causes of poor business communication. It will be extremely difficult to achieve your purpose if you don't know who your audience is—or you think you know but are mistaken.

There are two assumptions about the audience writers make all the time in business:

1. Everyone knows that.

2. They can figure it out.

Rarely is the assumption "everyone knows that" correct. Just because something is obvious to you doesn't mean it's obvious to everyone. With this attitude, you'll probably leave out important information—and leave readers in the dark. Assuming your audience knows something it doesn't is almost as bad as writing in a foreign language.

Nor is the assumption "they can figure it out" safe either. In fact, it's a dangerous assumption because readers don't want to have to figure it out. They expect you to explain it to them.

So how do you avoid making these costly assumptions? You get to know your audience.

Who is your audience, anyway? Are they managers, front-line employees, hourly or salary employees, employees in another country, human resources professionals? Sometimes your audience may be a group of strangers. Other times it may consist of individuals you know. This insight will determine your approach, the language you use, your tone, what you say and how you say it.

Could your audience be multi-level? You're likely—in business writing especially—to find that this is the case. For example, you may be writing an executive summary for management, the body copy for employees and an appendix for specialists. Or you may be writing all the sections so that all the audiences of your document can understand them. Or you may be writing each section for a specific audience and using headings and other formatting to let the audience know what to read and not read.

Is there variability in the background and experience of those in your audience?
Once again, in business writing this is often the case. Do you write to the lowest common denominator of reader? If you do, will you turn off the rest of your audience? Still, you don't want to lose that segment of low-level readers. You may find the best approach is to appeal to the majority of readers and include optional supplemental materials for the rest.

How much does your audience already know? Just knowing "who" your audience is isn't enough. You also need to analyze audience members in terms of different characteristics. What is their technical background? Do they have any strong opinions about the subject? Or biases? Why do they care? What have you learned through research interviews or other means about your readers that will help you connect with them? What do your readers want or need? What objections may each reader have? How will you overcome those objections?

What is their background and experience? How much knowledge, experience or training do your readers have? If you think some readers will have less experience than others, should you bring them up to speed? If you don't, will they get frustrated? If you do, will you lose the interest of the more experienced readers in your audience? The answers to these questions may not be easy. How can you get valuable background information on your audience? A tried and true way is through your first-hand experience—for example by conducting interviews.

What other characteristics do you need to know about? Many other factors may influence how your readers respond to your writing—including their age, the length of employment in your company and so on. Find out this information.

You Try It

Think of a document you've been meaning to write, but just can't get started on. Imagine you're writing to an actual person. Now describe six things you know about that person:

The person's position is: _____

The person's title is: _____

The person's profession/industry/field is: _____

The person is interested in my message because: _____

The person will use the information in this way: _____

The person already knows this about the topic: _____

Keep this specific person in mind as you write. This can help you make the right decisions about what information to include, how to present it and how to best support it.

Pitch Your Content to Your Audience's Readability Level

Like many writers, you've probably heard or been told that you need to aim at a low level when writing for the American audience. That's true—but not because Americans lack intelligence or education. They can comprehend writing beyond an 8th grade level. It's just that they won't bother because they are so incredibly busy. They don't have time to wade through complicated, confusing writing.

If your vocabulary, examples and assumed level of familiarity are off-base, you'll lose your reader. You need to take into account your audience's level of expertise, education, gender and cultural differences. Keep all these characteristics in mind as you write.

What reading level should you aim for? Studies suggest that the more frequently a reader must stop to reread or figure out what the writer meant, the more likely the reader is to give up and stop reading. So it's important to aim for the right reading level. The general rule is to write as if your reader is in the 8th grade. So make this your goal and you can't go wrong.

How do you measure the reading level of your audience? Numerous readability formulas have been developed to gauge the difficulty of written text. One of the most widely used is the Flesch Formula. It is the basis of the Microsoft® Word grammar checker. When Microsoft Word finishes checking the spelling and grammar, you can choose to display information about the reading level of the document, including readability scores according to the Flesch Formula for reading ease and grade level.

Or you can do it yourself:

The Flesch Formula: Reading Ease and Grade Level

1. Select a 100-word sample and count the number of sentences.

2. Divide the number of words (100) by the number of sentences and multiply the result by 1.015. Save this result and call it x.

3. Count the total number of syllables in the sample, divide by the total number of words (100) and multiply by 84.6 (or just multiply the number of syllables by 0.846—the results will be the same). Now call this number y.

4. Add x to y and subtract the sum from 206.835. The final result is the Reading Ease Score.

Check out your score:

- 0 – 29 Very Difficult Post-Graduate

- 30 – 49 Difficult College

- 50 – 59 Fairly Difficult High School

- 60 – 69 Standard 8th to 9th grade

- 70 – 79 Fairly Easy 7th grade

- 80 – 89 Easy 5th to 6th grade

- 90 – 100 Very Easy 4th to 5th grade

There are other ways to calculate the grade level of a writing sample:

- Fry Readability Graph

- SMOG Formula

- Gunning Fog Index

- SAM (Suitability Assessment of Materials)

You may also want to check out these readability software programs:

- Readability Plus (Windows® and Mac®)

- Readability Studio (Windows®)

- Stylewriter Plus (Windows® and Mac®)

What if you find your writing is missing your target?

Don't panic. You can do a number of things quickly and easily to make your writing more understandable:

1. *Eliminate information your audience doesn't need.* They won't read it anyway so why include it? Or if they do feel obligated to read it, it may confuse and frustrate them.

2. *Change your pitch.* You may have the right information but be aiming it too high or too low.

3. *Add examples to help readers understand.* When you're trying to explain a new concept or a concept unfamiliar to your audience, examples—especially analogies, where you compare one thing to another—can help you clarify your point.

4. *Re-organize your information.* You may have all the correct information, but it may be arranged in a way that confuses readers. For example, you may have placed too much detail at the beginning of the document, when it might be better to feed the reader this information in sections.

5. *Give readers the big picture in your introduction and subsections.* Your introduction should tell the reader what's ahead and clarify the topic, purpose and content of the document. Each subsection should include its own introduction to the topic that will be covered and tell how it relates to what the reader has already read.

6. *Adapt the style and length of sentences to the reader.* For example, personalizing your writing by frequently using "you" may make your message friendlier and more accessible. It's harder to make the connection when you use the third person. And avoid long sentences—regardless of your audience. By doing so, you'll undoubtedly eliminate fussy, unnecessary words that are frustrating to read and muddle your message.

7. *Break up the content into chunks.* Short paragraphs are easier to digest and less intimidating. Simply seeing a long, wordy paragraph may be enough to make your reader stop reading. Try breaking up dense paragraphs with subheads, lists and bullets. Look for changes in a topic or subtopic—that may be a good place to add a subhead. Think of what can be conveyed in a list.

Never Miss a Deadline: How to Write Under Pressure

Few of us have the luxury of writing whenever we feel like it or taking as long as we wish. Most of the time, we're expected to crank something out almost instantaneously. Yet you know first-hand how much time the writing process can take. You can spin your wheels for hours wondering where to begin … what to say … and exactly how to say it.

The next time you're facing a last-minute writing assignment, don't panic. You can do it. Journalists are constantly writing "breaking news" stories under deadline pressure. In fact, many writers find that the less time they have to write, the more productive they are. You can do this. You can write faster. All it takes is practice, good organizational skills and—of course—a stopwatch.

Here are 12 tips for writing under pressure without stressing out:

1. *Analyze what it is you need to write.* What is your purpose? Who is your audience? What do you want them to do? It should take you only a few minutes to answer these questions.

2. *Write one sentence that summarizes your purpose.* Everything that follows should refer back to this purpose.

3. *Create a plan of action.* Make a list of questions you need to answer and details you must include.

4. *Set a deadline.* How much time do you have to complete the writing? Knowing this will help you manage your time wisely.

5. *Establish a timetable.* Decide how much time you'll spend on each part of the task.

6. *Create an outline.* Put the points that need to be addressed in logical order. Fill in each point with as many details as you can.

7. *Begin writing.* Turn your points into sentences. Try writing bullets and numbered lists instead of paragraphs. You reader will be able to skim your writing quickly to find information they need or want.

8. *Skip around.* If you get stuck writing one part, move on to the next. Then go back.

9. *Write the introduction last.* It's fine to put this off. Pull out the main ideas you've already written about and summarize them in an introductory statement.

10. *Read over what you've written.* Check for any mistakes in spelling, grammar, facts or details. This is your opportunity to make sure everything is correct.

11. *If time permits, write another draft.* Correct any problems you found when proofreading. Polish your writing as much as you can.

12. *Skip the writing altogether.* If you can pick up the phone and call, by all means do! Talking may be more effective if you're giving feedback, discussing confidential information, resolving a conflict, establishing a new relationship with someone or presenting an idea that may not be immediately accepted.

You Try It

Here's a worksheet to fill out the next time you're facing a short turnaround time.

Deadline: _____

What is the purpose? (Limit this to one sentence.) _____

_____

Who is the audience? _____

_____

What do you want them to do? _____

_____

What questions will they have that you need to answer?

1. _____

2. _____

3. _____

What points do you need to address? List them in logical order:

1. _____

2. _____

3. _____

What points must be in your introduction?

1. _____

2. _____

3. _____

CHAPTER TWO

Getting Your
First Draft
on Paper

If you think you're the only person who struggles with getting a first draft on paper, relax. You're not alone. Getting started is hard. But there are ways to make the grueling process easier—and even fun.

Overcome Writer's Block

Are you one of those people who can find a million other things to do when it's time to sit down and write? You clean your desk, organize your files, line up your pens, answer every e-mail in your inbox and do whatever else you can to avoid putting pen to paper. Let's face it. Writing is not an activity that most people love. In fact, many take every opportunity to not even start a writing project because they find writing so difficult. Here we'll discuss some ways you can overcome writer's block and see writing as the simple task it is—and one you can learn to do well.

What is writer's block, exactly? Writer's block happens when you aren't sure what to write or where to begin. You may get it when you lack sleep … feel stressed … or secretly fear failure—or success. Unlike with arthritis or strep throat, there are no medical tests that will prove you have writer's block. You know you have it because you simply don't want to write. What to do? There are many suggested cures. Some writers will swear by one method and others will insist another works. Here are some ideas you can try to get you over the hump:

1. *Close the door and turn off the phone.* You need periods of uninterrupted time if you are to make any progress.

2. *Talk it out with a friend or colleague.* So often, saying it out loud helps your ideas crystallize.

3. *Experiment.* Try writing in a different location or at a different time. Write longhand if you usually type or vice versa.

4. *Walk around.* Stretch. Go get a cup of coffee or tea or a soft drink.

5. *Lower your standards.* Your first draft does *not* have to be perfect. Your boss or other "critics" won't see your work until it's final. So don't worry about being judged.

6. *Skip the part that's bugging you.* Just make a note to yourself to go back. Go on to an easier part. Meanwhile let your subconscious mind work on it.

7. *Don't quit.* You'll be tempted to stop when writing feels like a struggle. But keep plugging along. Inspiration comes in spurts. You've got to be there to catch it.

How About You?

Feeling blocked? Check which of the below statements describe why you can't get started:

- ☐ I don't know what I want to say.
- ☐ I don't feel inspired.
- ☐ I'm not sure how.
- ☐ I can't—I'm really not a writer.
- ☐ I feel the first draft must be perfect.
- ☐ I'm really not interested in the topic.
- ☐ I'm afraid others will react negatively.

Now think about the solutions just discussed. Describe which of those you plan to try:

_____

_____

_____

Start the Engines With Free-writing

You're sitting at your computer. The screen is blank. You have to finish a performance evaluation or a hiring recommendation or some other document by 5 p.m. and you're feeling stressed. You thought you knew exactly what you need to say. But now you're not sure. You have a lot of information and thoughts swirling around in your head—and no idea how to organize them or get them down on paper.

If your ideas are tangled in your mind and you simply don't know how to make sense of them, try free-writing to jump-start the writing process. Free-writing is a fast and easy way to gather your thoughts and ideas on a topic. It involves continuous writing in short bursts for a set period of time. You don't think about it. You just go to your keyboard and write. Write about the topic if you can. If you can't, just write about anything.

Why does free-writing work? It reminds you of what you already know and helps you make connections you might not otherwise make. You're not expected to turn out letter-perfect work when free-writing. The point is to gather your thoughts and ideas and produce an endless, non-punctuated paragraph that will help launch the real process of writing. It may seem silly at first, but don't give up after one try. Keep working at it. With practice, you'll get better at it. It may even become liberating. And, as it is for many business professionals, it could become a method you use every day.

How to free-write:

- *Select a topic*—such as the writing task you're facing at the moment.

- *Start a timer.* Give yourself 5 to 10 minutes to continuously write.

- *Write down whatever comes to mind.* If it's related to your topic, that's fine. If it's not, that's okay too. The idea is to write down every thought that crosses your mind as quickly as possible. If you run into a dead-end or draw a blank, keep writing the same word or phrase over and over again until something else pops into your mind.

- *Keep writing until the timer goes off.* No longer.

- *Look over what you've written.* Highlight or underline thoughts that may be useful for your project. Write one sentence that summarizes your main point. Repeat this process several times and your most important ideas will emerge.

- *Group the ideas you've marked* and decide where they lead you in your writing process.

- *Start writing your first draft.* It won't be nearly as hard as you thought.

Here are 11 tips for making free-writing work:

1. *Don't think*—just write whatever comes into your head.

2. *Keep writing*, even if you have to write "I don't know what to write."

3. *Don't judge or evaluate what you write.* Do not cross anything out.

4. *Use a pen, computer*—whatever works for you.

5. *Do not correct spelling or punctuation or check facts as you write.*

6. *Don't worry about incomplete sentences.* You can always go back and finish them.

7. *Get messy.* If your free-writing is too orderly, you probably haven't loosened up enough.

8. *Let your mind wander.* Your best ideas may come when you allow your mind to get out of the way.

9. *Don't read what you've written* until you are finished.

10. *Read your free-writing to yourself out loud.* You may be pleasantly surprised when you pick up an idea or two you hadn't noticed when you were free-writing.

11. *Read your free-writing to a co-worker* or ask the co-worker to read it to you.

How About You?

Is free-writing for you? Check which of the below statements you can identify with:

- ☐ I need help getting comfortable with writing.
- ☐ I'm looking for a way to shut down those "inner voices" that say I can't write.
- ☐ I'm tense. I need to loosen up.
- ☐ I wish there were a way I could warm up for the writing process.
- ☐ I need to clear my mind—I have a thousand thoughts swirling around and I can't concentrate.
- ☐ I need to find a new way to look at the topic.
- ☐ I'm in the middle of my document and am feeling stuck. I need to get back on track.

Why not give free-writing a try? You have nothing to lose.

Mindmap to Organize Your Ideas

Writing calls for good organizational skills. You have to be able to gather countless random ideas, sort through them and put them in a logical order the reader can easily understand. When your ideas are well-organized, you should be ready to write. Mindmapping is a simple technique that helps you go through the ideas you generate and organize them.

A mindmap is a flow chart of the information you want to convey about a specific topic. The technique involves creating a tree-like structure that helps you get a better handle on your information and organize your thoughts. Try it the next time you need to develop a meeting agenda, write a memo or get a big-picture view of a complex subject. It should take only a few minutes.

How to mindmap:

- *Write your topic in the center of the page.*

- *Draw branches out from that topic* and write in keywords or phrases associated with the main topic.

- *Draw branches from the keywords and phrases* and develop each a little more.

- *Draw lines between the ideas* that could work together.

- *Decide if you want to regroup ideas.*

- *Do this as many times as necessary* until you have clear ideas you can work from.

Here are 13 tips for successful mindmapping:

1. *Eliminate all distractions.* Shut the door so you won't be disturbed.

2. *Start with a precisely defined idea.* This will help you focus on the goal.

3. *Try using a photo or image*—instead of a word—in the center of your mindmap.

4. *Write down every thought or idea* that comes to you.

5. *Don't worry if your ideas are all over the place.* You can make sense of them and that's what counts.

6. *Let loose.* Don't restrict yourself.

7. *Have extra paper handy* in case you want to expand your map.

8. *Forget about spelling, punctuation and grammar.* Worry about that later.

9. *Set a time limit.* This will get the creative juices flowing.

10. *Push yourself.* Even after you think you've exhausted all your ideas, take a fresh look at what you have written. Then push yourself a little harder to come up with more.

11. *Change the scenery.* Sometimes your environment may hold you back. Try doing your mindmapping someplace new—like at a coffee shop or in a park.

12. *Keep writing.* Don't stop. Your pen should be touching paper at all times.

13. *Have fun!*

When you get serious about using mindmapping for planning, brainstorming, scheduling and project management, try the software that was developed specifically for this purpose, MindMapper®.

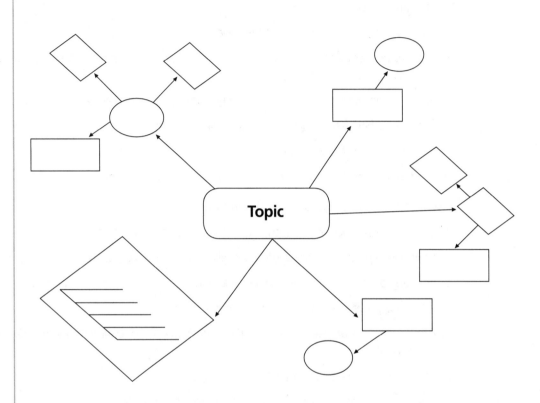

Topic

You Try It

Look at your schedule and pick up a writing project coming up that you fear you may struggle with. Use this template to mindmap your ideas. Start by writing the topic in the center of the page. Then follow the steps described earlier.

Structure Your Ideas Using the Inverted Pyramid

The foundation of all clear business writing is structure. You may not see it, but it's there. Whether you're writing a letter, an e-mail or any other type of document, the way you structure information directly affects how fast you get your message across. Here's a tip from the newsroom: Use the journalist's inverted pyramid structure.

With this method, you present the most essential information first and follow with supporting details in order of importance. By the end of the first paragraph—and at least by the end of the second—readers should have a clear idea of your point. If you want to be sure your writing is read by busy professionals, this is an effective structure to use. Your readers will appreciate it because it enables them to quit reading at any point and still come away with the essence of your document.

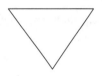

Think of the inverted pyramid as an upside-down triangle. The broad base is where the most important information appears. The narrow tip is where the least important information appears. When you use the inverted pyramid to structure your document, you decide where to start and finish, how to address your topic and what the logical conclusion is. Through this process you can learn a lot. You may discover you don't have a clear purpose. Or maybe you only make two points to support it. Or perhaps you don't reach any conclusions. By structuring your thoughts, you know where to focus when revising.

Here's how to write in inverted pyramid style:

- *Start with the key point of your message.* This should reflect the reason why you are writing and grab your audience's attention. Ask a question, pose a problem—whatever it takes to capture the reader's interest before their phone rings or the boss interrupts them.

- *Present the most pertinent details.* This is where you put in all the relevant information. To draw from the newsroom again, be sure you have the 5 Ws covered—who, what, when, where and why.

- *Add any supporting information.* Prioritize these points in descending order of importance. Invariably some information must be left out because there is simply not enough space.

Here's a newspaper article written in the inverted pyramid style. Imagine that you knew nothing about this event. Within the first two paragraphs, you would have learned virtually everything you need to know.

1. In the first paragraph, what did you learn?

2. In the second paragraph, what did you learn?

Tax rebates by direct deposit begin
By WILLIAM COLE
The Kansas City Register

About 7.7 million rebate payments had been sent to taxpayers by the end of last week, the Internal Revenue Service said.

More than 5 million payments went out on Friday, said IRS spokesman Michael Devine. The payments were being sent first to taxpayers who requested a direct deposit in their bank accounts.

The process was working smoothly, Devine said, but the IRS was receiving more inquiries than initially expected.

Many questions are from taxpayers, including Social Security recipients and disabled veterans, who have nontaxable income and so don't normally file a return. But this year, taxpayers who made at least $3,000 in earned income—whether taxable or not—will get rebate checks if they file a return.

The first paper checks will be dispatched by mail this Friday, Devine said.

The order of sending out payments is determined by the last two digits of a person's Social Security number. Taxpayers with numbers ending in 00 to 20 and who elected to receive their payments electronically should have seen the payments in their bank accounts by Saturday.

In all, payments totaling more than $110 billion are being sent to about 130 million households. All qualifying taxpayers need to do to get a stimulus rebate check is file a return.

Most Americans who are required to file returns can qualify for a payment of up to $600 for an individual and $1,200 for a married couple. Americans not required to file a return can qualify for up to $300, and $600 for a married couple. There also is a payment of $300 for each qualifying child younger than 17.

Write Your First Draft Faster

Writing the first draft is actually a late stage in the writing process. By the time you write your first draft, you will have already done some important preparation. You may have gathered your ideas through free-writing, sorted through them through mindmapping and given them structure using the inverted pyramid. The word "first" is important—there may likely be several drafts before you have a finished document you are happy with. Or, if your ideas are well-thought out, you may get the job done by editing the first draft.

Your goal when writing the first draft should be to get your ideas on paper and expand them. It may be hard to believe, but writing the first draft should be the least time-consuming part of the writing process. It should take less time than free-writing, mindmapping and writing an outline. And revising should definitely take longer.

Three types of drafts:

1. *Down-and-dirty draft.* You just get something on paper. It may be boring, long or disorganized.

2. *Fix-it-up draft.* You go back to the first draft and try to say what you have to say more clearly and accurately.

3. *Nail-it-down draft.* You polish, tweak, refine and improve until you get it right.

Here are 11 tips for writing your first draft:

1. *Just do it.* Don't wait until you feel inspired. Start writing.

2. *Work during your personal peak time.* Pick a time when you will feel fresh. Too often writers procrastinate until the end of the day, when they're tired and can't think clearly.

3. *Have everything you need nearby.* That includes your free-writing, mindmap, outline and any other materials you may need to refer to—such as numbers, facts or statistics. With all your resources nearby, you won't have to get up and get anything— and run the risk of losing your concentration.

4. *Create the best environment.* Shut the door. Forward your phone. Clear everything off your desk. If you need to, leave and go to the library, conference room or someplace else more conducive to writing than your office.

5. *Write as quickly as you can.* Try to get as many ideas down on paper as fast as you can. Don't worry about what you put down at this stage. You can change it later. Even if you repeat yourself and your ideas, it's okay. You can revise. It's just a first draft.

6. *Start with the easiest part.* That may be the middle. Or even the end.

7. *Write the first draft in one go.* Don't fuss or worry over any particular part. Just write.

8. *Don't worry about your opening.* You can really get stuck at the starting gate if you do. Some people write many different openings, reject them, start over and waste time. It's fine to leave the opening until your second draft.

9. *Don't stop to find missing material.* This will halt your progress. Simply make a note in parentheses and add the information later. Then move on.

10. *Don't stop to check spelling, correct punctuation and look up facts.* You can't write and edit at the same time. Each task involves different parts of your brain. Your goal is to just get words on paper. If you stop you may lose your train of thought or run out of time. Simply underline or highlight the areas you think are wrong. You can go back later and fix them.

11. *Write in whatever way works for you.* You may feel most comfortable typing it. But if you prefer to write it out in longhand, that's fine too. Many writers find that after writing in longhand, the process of entering it into their computer enables them to more easily see what needs to be changed.

You Try It

Use this space to list things that in the last week have kept you from writing your first draft as quickly as you needed to. For example: I was continually interrupted by the phone.

1._____

2._____

3._____

4._____

5._____

Now take some time to reflect on the above list.

- What can you learn from this?

- In the next week, try to be aware of these barriers.

- What can you do about them?

CHAPTER THREE

Writing Clearly
and Concisely
for Today's
Busy Readers

Reading is hard work. The typical businessperson has only so much brainpower they are willing to devote to deciphering a memo, letter or report. Your job must be to convey your message in the clearest and simplest way possible so readers don't have to struggle to read it, but understand it the first time through.

Construct Crisp and Clear Sentences

If you think you need to impress people by stringing together a bunch of fancy words in one long sentence, forget it. Brevity is truly a virtue—especially when it comes to writing sentences. Writing long sentences is a habit you can get into without even realizing it. However, help is on the way. It's a handy punctuation mark called the period. Put a period at the end of your sentences. Stop when you've said enough. Like this.

In business writing, try to keep sentences no longer than 12 words. And be sure to mix in some short sentences to add emphasis. Your writing will be clear and readable if you do.

Here are eight tips for putting sentences on a diet:

1. *Limit each sentence to one idea.* Simple sentences are easy to understand. Usually a simple sentence contains one subject and one verb. If you write a sentence that's too complex, it's going to be difficult to understand without effort on the reader's part.

2. *Avoid too-long sentences.* Break long sentences into shorter ones. Beware of stringing thoughts together with "and."

3. *Vary the length of sentences.* Don't bore your readers by structuring every sentence in the same way. Or writing sentences all the same length. Spice it up.

4. *Do not start with "There are."* Sometimes it's effective to begin a sentence with "there" or "there are." However, use this approach sparingly because it makes writing clumsy. Begin each sentence strong.

   BEFORE: "There are many employees who donated to the fund."

   AFTER: "Many employees donated to the fund."

5. *Use the active, not passive, voice.* In sentences written in the active voice, the subject performs the action expressed in the verb. Sometimes writing in the passive voice causes awkward sentences. Overuse of the passive voice makes writing dull and uninteresting.

   BEFORE: "The prize was won by Linda."

   AFTER: "Linda won the prize."

6. *Don't back into the sentence.* The end of the sentence is where the most important information should appear.

   BEFORE: "The lack of sales in the first quarter of the year and the suggested remedies are the subject of this meeting."

   AFTER: "The purpose of this meeting is to discuss the lack of sales in the first quarter of the year and suggested remedies."

7. *Use parallel construction.* In parallel construction, words and phrases are used in like ways within the same sentence.

   BEFORE: "Tom enjoys supervising employees, training new hires and project management."

   AFTER: "Tom enjoys supervising employees, training new hires and managing projects."

8. *Make sure every sentence adds something new.* In fact, every phrase and clause should add something new.

You Try It

Rewrite each of the following sentences to achieve a concise statement:

Basically, in light of the fact that the employee had many years of experience managing technical projects, there was an expectation that she would meet performance objectives more quickly than she did.

Your rewrite: _____

_____

_____

_____

At this point in time, there is no solution to the budget problem.

Your rewrite: _____

_____

_____

_____

My boss, who chairs the committee and is a major supporter of recycling in both homes and businesses, recommends each person attend the seminar.

Your rewrite: _____

_____

_____

_____

There is an interest among many of today's IT professionals to pursue a service-oriented architecture in order to cut costs and improve productivity.

Your rewrite: _____

_____

_____

_____

At the present time, there is no indication that a change in marketing strategy will hurt the bottom line as a whole.

Your rewrite: _____

_____

_____

_____

Create a Logical Road Map With Paragraphs

Your readers don't know where they're going—you have to show them. Paragraphs are a great tool for doing just that. What constitutes a paragraph? Not length. A paragraph is a collection of sentences created around one main idea. Everything in the paragraph supports that controlling idea. Think of your paragraphs as tied together by a string. One leads into the next. Together they provide a logical road map for your readers.

Whether you are writing about something simple or complicated, paragraphs can help you present your ideas logically—in an order in which your readers would think through and assimilate new ideas. You build your document paragraph by paragraph. Start with what readers know. Take them to the next idea. Then lead them to the next and so on.

You can improve the flow of your writing by linking paragraphs with transition words and phrases, for example:

- Next …
- In addition …
- However …
- Another …
- For example …
- Besides …
- Finally …

They serve as bridges from one idea to the next, one sentence to the next, one paragraph to the next. They help readers make logical connections between paragraphs. They function as signs that keep readers from getting lost or confused.

You may need to work on your transitions if you've ever been told—or you think—your writing is choppy … doesn't flow well … jumps from one idea to another. Or if you write documents in chunks and then tie them together. Or if readers frequently say they had trouble following your thinking or logic. Or if you write the way you think and your thinking tends to be disorganized.

Three types of transitions:

1. *Between sections.* Let's say you are writing a report divided into several different sections. At the end of each section you'll need to write a statement that summarizes the section just concluded and tells how it relates to the next section.

2. *Between paragraphs.* Ideally you have written paragraphs that flow logically from one to the next. You can use a transition like "however" or "moreover" at the beginning of the paragraph for greater clarity.

3. *Within paragraphs.* By using a simple word or phrase, you can alert readers to what's coming next in the paragraph.

Transitional expressions can also be used to:

- Show how two ideas are similar: "also, in the same way, likewise"

- Contrast ideas: "however, nonetheless, in spite of"

- Sequence ideas: "first, second, next, finally"

- Give a time reference: "before, currently, earlier, recently"

- Emphasize: "in fact, truly, indeed"

- Show place or position: "beyond, nearby, behind"

- Show cause and effect: "so, consequently, thus"

- Provide additional evidence: "equally important, in addition, moreover"

- Conclude or summarize: "in the end, finally, to summarize"

Here are five tips for writing effective paragraphs:

1. *Focus on one idea in each paragraph.* Each paragraph should be constructed around a single idea that relates back to your key message. It's better to have three paragraphs than to cram three ideas with no relationship to each other into one.

2. *Limit the length of each paragraph.* Why? Because you need to be concerned about your reader's first impression. If the page looks like a blob of unbroken type, your reader may give up and not even try to read it.

3. *Start a new paragraph when you begin a new idea or you contrast information or ideas.* Or when your reader needs a break because the material has become too complex or long or you are ready to conclude.

4. *Vary the length of paragraphs.* Every once in a while, use a one-sentence paragraph for impact. Add in a few two- and three-sentence paragraphs and you should be just fine. You'll keep your document from looking dull and your readers from getting bored. This is especially true in long or technical documents.

5. *Be logical.* Organize paragraphs in order of importance or in chronological order. Use a logical system of headings and subheadings to help readers understand and follow the order.

You Try It

How many ways can you find to improve this paragraph?

A-Plus is totally committed to providing you with a thorough proposal for a zoning system as opposed to simply giving you a bid. In fact, we avoid using the term bid as it implies that every company is providing you with the same products and benefits and future service thereby making price the only deciding criteria. That said, our goal is not to be the least expensive but rather provide you with an unparalleled professional install while at the same time maintaining a relentlessly high level of customer service.

Choose the Shortest Word Necessary to Communicate Your Meaning

You may want to wow others with your command of the English language and vast vocabulary, but your writing is not the place to do so. Words that are misused, inappropriate, misplaced, overblown and imprecise all add up to a big clarity problem.

Use short words that are easy to read and understand. If you're afraid readers will think your writing is too simplistic, fear not. Readers will not only be more likely to read what you've written, but they will probably read the whole thing, understand what it is you want them to do and then do it.

Every once in a while, you will probably need to write a formal letter using formal language. But most of the time you'll find you can replace every complicated word with a simpler one. What is a complicated word? That's easy. If the word makes your reader stop and wonder "Huh?" then it needs to be replaced.

Simple is better. The people who write traffic signs got it right:

- One way
- Stop
- Merge
- Do not enter
- Slow down

Power Tip:

For every 100 words you write, make sure that 75 of them are words of five letters or less.

Here are five tips for choosing lean words:

1. *Avoid ten-dollar words.* Choose words with one or two syllables. Abraham Lincoln's Gettysburg Address contains 275 words—and 196 of those words have only one syllable!

   See the difference?

   - Gather, not accumulate
   - Use, not utilize
   - Show, not manifest
   - First, not initial
   - Likely, not feasible
   - Guess, not conjecture
   - Expect, not anticipate
   - Follow, not adhere to

2. *Use only words you can pronounce.* If you stumble over the pronunciation, chances are you're unsure of the meaning and your readers may be too.

   Don't use:

   - Cacophony
   - Macabre
   - Despot
   - Debacle
   - Cache
   - Paradigm
   - Exacerbate

3. *Attack adverbs and adjectives.* Too often adverbs and adjectives are not necessary. If they don't add substantial meaning, ax them:

   - Truly overdone
   - Somewhat interesting
   - Totally unreasonable

4. *Avoid words that end in "ion" or "ness."* Usually you can drop these endings and turn lifeless nouns into strong verbs or adjectives.

Which word sounds stronger?

- Carefulness or careful?

- Conclusion or conclude?

- Consideration or consider?

- Modification or modify?

5. *Avoid stuffy words and language.* You see this often in business—language that is pompous, old-fashioned and pretentious. Avoid it unless there is some compelling reason to use it.

Don't use:

- Per your request

- To effectuate

- Conceptualization

- Methodology

You Try It

You may find it difficult to limit most of your words to five letters. It takes practice. But it's worth it.

1. Select a sample of a letter you wrote. Count the number of words.

2. Forget about any proper nouns, the salutation and the closing. Just focus on the body copy.

3. Count how many words you used that contain five letters or less.

4. Divide this total by the total number of words.

My score: _____

What your score means:

- 75% or so … that's good

- Below 70% … your writing is more difficult for your reader to understand than necessary

---

Be on the Alert for Inappropriate Language

When writing, it's important to use language that fits your audience. Inappropriate language can turn off a reader, damage your credibility and alienate people. For example, slang and jargon are useful in getting your message across only if your audience understands what you mean.

Here are six tips for eliminating inappropriate language:

1. *Leave out jargon.*

    Jargon is terminology that relates to a specific industry or group. It's kind of like slang. Like clichés, jargon is frequently used in writing. This is fine if the readers understand it. If you're not sure, leave it out.

    Don't use:

    - Shareware
    - Third generation
    - Right sized
    - Bandwidth
    - C-level
    - Brush fire
    - Critical path
    - Deliverables
    - Dialogue
    - Hired gun
    - Drill-down
    - Functionality
    - Mission critical

2. *Be sure to define acronyms.*

   Using acronyms is a popular and widely accepted practice in business. Acronyms enable you to avoid repeating long words and phrases over and over. But if the acronym is unfamiliar to the reader it will mean nothing, so the first time you use one, write out what it stands for, either before or after the acronym. Put whichever form comes second in parentheses, for example:

   UNICEF (United Nations International Children's Emergency Fund)

   Federal Trade Commission (FTC)

3. *Put worn-out clichés to rest.*

   A cliché is a word, phrase or expression that is so overused it has lost its meaning. Yes, readers get what you mean. They've heard the saying over and over. But it makes your writing flat when it could sparkle. The use of clichés may also suggest a bit of laziness on the writer's part. You will no doubt get to your point more quickly without them. How do you find clichés? Question the use of any comparison or image. If you hear it frequently in conversation or on TV, it may be a cliché. Practice spotting clichés used in everyday conversations. You'll probably notice there are many. Read your work out loud and any clichés you missed in editing will come to light.

   Examples of popular clichés:

   - Fresh as a daisy
   - Pull out all the stops
   - You can't win them all
   - The name of the game
   - Work smarter, not harder
   - Put our heads together

4. *Avoid biased language.*

   Avoid using any language that is stereotypical in any way. Biased language often refers to gender but can also refer to race, age, religion or sexual orientation. Biased words and phrases cause a reader to focus on how you say something rather than on what you say. Instead use language that is inclusive and not offensive.

   See how this language is biased?

   - "A president must keep his focus on unity."
   - "A black man knocked on the door."
   - "Even though Mary is 62, she can still do the job."

5. *Purge your writing of sexist language.*

The word "man" originally meant both adult human and adult male. But its meaning has come to be so closely identified with adult male only that the generic use of "man" and other words with a masculine connotation should be avoided.

Don't use:	Use:
Layman	Layperson
Salesgirl	Sales assistant
Workman	Worker
Chairman	Chair, chairperson, head
Policeman	Police officer
Stewardess	Flight attendant
Spokesman	Spokesperson
Mothering	Nurturing
Average man	Average person

Another problem is that the English language has no generic singular—or common-sex—pronoun. Frequently the words "he," "him" and "his" are used if the sex of a person is not specified. When you constantly personify others as male even though they are not by using the pronoun *he*, you are excluding women.

Here are several alternatives to the use of masculine pronouns:

Original:	Alternative:
Give each employee his paycheck by the end of the day.	Give employees their paychecks by the end of the day.
The typical employee is worried about his future.	The typical employee is worried about the future.
Let each employee speak. Has he had the opportunity to express his opinion? Could he feel left out?	Let each employee speak. Has she had the opportunity to express her opinion? Could he feel left out?
Anyone who wants to go to the company picnic should bring his money tomorrow.	All those who want to go to the company picnic should bring their money tomorrow.

6. *Use euphemisms with care.*

A euphemism is an agreeable word or phrase substituted for a word or phrase some might find offensive. Sometimes a euphemism is appropriate (for example, "passed away" is an acceptable substitution for "died" in some situations), but it's generally a good idea to use the more literal word or phrase.

For example, use:

- "Pregnant" instead of "in the family way"
- "Men's restroom" instead of "little boys' room"

You Try It

Rewrite these sentences by replacing the inappropriate language (noted in parentheses):

We promise our product is (second to none).

Your rewrite without clichés: _____

_____

_____

_____

An attorney experienced in this specific area of law is (worth (his) weight in gold).

Your rewrite without sexist language or clichés: _____

_____

_____

_____

I hope you can (resolve this issue) because we don't have time (to revisit it).

Your rewrite with lean words: _____

_____

_____

_____

Whenever possible, (proof) a (hard copy) of a document.

Your rewrite without jargon: _____

_____

_____

_____

Clear Out the Clutter

When writing and editing, your goal should be to eliminate any unnecessary words from sentences. Ask yourself: Does this word help me make my point? Or does it detract from clarity? Don't waste space on unnecessary words.

Here are five tips for clearing out the clutter:

1. *Don't use a phrase when a single word will do.*

Wordy	Trim
At the present time	Now
In the event of	If
In the majority of cases	Usually
Submit an application for	Apply
Implement an investigation of	Investigate
Conduct a review of	Review
A certain number of	Some
Within the framework of	Under
With reference to	About
Basic fundamentals	Basic
To all appearances	Apparently
With confidence	Confidently
For the most part	Usually
A possibility that	Possibly

2. *Delete redundancies.*

   Repetitious expressions are seen a lot in business writing, so they're easy to overlook. But they are not necessary to make a point. In the following examples, the words in parentheses can be omitted and the meaning will be the same:

   - (Advance) warning
   - ATM (machine)
   - (Brief) summary
   - Circulate (around)
   - Close (down)
   - (Exact) replica
   - Emergency (situation)
   - (Exactly) alike
   - (Active) consideration
   - (Past) history
   - Visible (to the eye)
   - Refer (back)
   - Repeat (again)
   - (Integral) part

3. *Get rid of throat-clearers.*

   These empty phrases at the beginning of sentences add nothing but words to your writing.

   - In order to
   - For the reason that
   - There is
   - With a view to
   - In terms of

4. *Cut all intensifiers.*

Frequently, writers will modify or quantify words that don't need to be modified or quantified. Intensifiers add little to the meaning of your sentence.

- Absolutely perfect
- Perfectly clear
- Completely accurate

5. *Replace corporate mush.*

These are worn out terms and phrases you hear so often, they've lost their impact.

- Leverage
- User-friendly
- Proactive

You Try It

Pull a few memos or letters you or someone else has written. Read each one line by line. With a highlighter, note areas where there is clutter. Watch for redundant words and phrases, corporate mush, intensifiers and throat-clearers. Rewrite the documents eliminating the clutter.

Format for Readability

Do these two types of readers sound familiar?

- **Skimmers** who have little time to read—so they scan business documents to quickly pick up the key points

- **Skeptics** who read a document carefully but are doubtful about the message—so they need to be convinced about the writer's credibility and claims

How can you write so that both skimmers and skeptics read all the way to the end of your document, understand it and act upon it? You have to format your document so it can be easily skimmed and can easily convince the reader. Don't overlook the power of visual elements like bullets, lists, charts, subheads and pull-quotes. They can help you organize your information, capture your reader's attention and point to what's most important.

Power Tip:

The reality is that readers may look at only these visual elements. Nothing else. If that's the case—and you must assume it will be—these elements must tell the whole story.

A document that has a strong visual format eliminates confusion. For example, if three requirements need to be satisfied before a proposal will work, present those three requirements in a single list. Don't sprinkle them throughout your work so that it's harder for your reader to find them.

Here are 10 tips for improving readability with formatting:

1. *Use headings to tell the reader what's coming.* They'll direct the reader through your writing, help organize the page and make skimming your message easy. Keep headings around 4 – 8 words. Choose no more than two font styles—for example, use bold for the main headings and italics for subheads.

2. *Arrange information in bullet points and lists.* Bullets are typographical symbols—such as boxes, dashes and checkmarks—that organize information in a list format. If you have a long sentence, see if it can be broken down into a list. Limit each list to a dozen or so items. Use numbers where the order is important. Use bullets where the order doesn't matter. Introduce each list with at least one line of text.

3. *Use boldface to emphasize.* Don't overdo this. If you make too many areas bold, the reader will think none of them are important.

4. *Leave ample white space.* This will make your page more inviting and create the impression that it is easy to read. Allow at least one inch margins on all sides.

5. *Use a serif font* that adds visual impact. Times New Roman is a popular business font. Don't go overboard on fonts or your page will look cluttered. Stick to two or so.

6. *Limit the length of paragraphs.* If they're too long, your page will look text-heavy and intimidating. There's no hard-and-fast rule about paragraph length—use your own visual judgment.

7. *Use a font size of 12* so the text is large enough to read without a struggle.

8. *Avoid using all caps, underlining too much or putting large blocks of text in italics.* You don't want to make the text difficult to read.

9. *Use charts and graphs* instead of wasting space explaining. A simple line or bar chart with a descriptive title can quickly convey a message that would take you paragraphs to explain in words.

10. *Use pull-quotes*—small pieces of the text pulled and repeated in larger font size—to call certain information to the attention of the reader.

CHAPTER
FOUR
Developing a Style That
Instantly Connects
You With Readers

Style is the way you put words and phrases together when you write. It flows from how you speak and think. You have your own natural writing style too, even if you don't realize it. Does your writing style reveal your personality—who you really are? Do you speak quickly, loudly, forcefully, softly? Does your writing come across the same way? That's the style you want to capitalize on. When you let the real you come through in your writing, you sound more authentic, people connect with you more easily and you get better results.

Let Your Personality Leap off the Page

Your writing style—like the way you dress—flows from your personality. You are unique. There's no other writer in the world like you. Don't be afraid to let your personality leap off the page. When you do, your readers will feel they're talking to a real person. They'll be more likely to trust you and feel comfortable with you than if you were trying to be somebody you're not.

It's common for writers to elevate their style of writing to try to impress others. But that usually comes across as fake. Try to just be yourself. Don't try so hard to be clever or different. If you find you're using words that don't fit your style … if you're straining to achieve a certain tone … if you're looking for your thesaurus every few minutes … step back for a moment and remember: Writing is about honest communication. Use language that you're comfortable with and your readers will feel comfortable too.

When somebody meets you in person, they quickly pick up on your personality. Even when you're talking with someone on the phone, the real you shines through. And you'll likely be remembered for that. Writing is different. You have to make a serious effort to let your personality shine through. But few business professionals recognize the value of that. They hide behind stiff, academic words. They proceed cautiously because they don't want to offend anyone by breaking "the rules." As a result, they fail to release their personality, they come across as robot-like and they don't connect with their readers—so they're quickly forgotten.

Here are 11 tips for letting your personality shine through:

1. *Show who you are.* You can convey many feelings and attitudes through your writing—serious, casual, funny or professional to name a few.

2. *Read everything you write out loud,* as if you were giving a speech before thousands of people. Does it sound like you?

3. *Listen to the way your personality is expressed in everyday conversations.* Watch for certain words and phrases you use frequently. Now, weave those into your writing. If you need to use sophisticated words to get your point across, do so—but sparingly.

4. *Follow the rules—but don't be rigid.* Careful grammar and punctuation still matter. But don't try too hard to write "correctly" or you may drown in the rules.

5. *Don't wing it.* You still need to plan what you're going to write and how.

6. *Don't try to write like someone else.* Be yourself. You want your document to read like a real person—not some announcer without a personality.

7. *Experiment with different voices.* Find out what feels right for you. When you read a document that's flat and cardboard-like, you can be certain the writer's voice is absent. This happens for several different reasons. The writer either doesn't care about the topic or doesn't thoroughly understand the subject or how to approach it.

8. *Let your passion guide you.* If you're excited about what you're writing about, it will come through. Let it.

9. *Let yourself go.* If you concentrate on every single word you write, you'll lose your flow. Relax.

10. *Use strong, active verbs.* Passive language sounds more formal.

11. *Develop a rhythm to your writing.* Use periods, commas and other punctuation to establish it. Mark a shift in thinking by starting a new paragraph or using a transition word.

Write Like You Talk and Then Edit

It used to be that all business writing was formal—even stuffy. Not any longer. Along with dress codes, writing has become a lot more relaxed. Most of the time, you want your writing to come across as natural, personal—just as if you were having a conversation across the desk with a colleague or your boss. To make this happen, don't use fancy words you wouldn't normally use in a conversation. Or long sentences. Or formal language that is stiff. Of course, you don't want to sound too casual and irritate readers. But readers may want to be entertained while you're feeding them the information they need to know.

Writing is about getting your point across without the benefit of body language or vocal inflections. In most cases, you're better off writing documents using a natural, conversational style. When you write using a conversational style, readers are more likely to read, understand and remember what you write. They're more likely to feel like they know you and will more quickly trust you.

Some people naturally write like they talk. For others, it's not so easy. How do you know if you're coming across like you talk? Listen to yourself. Read something you've written out loud. Listen to the sound of the words. You can make them sound even better with some editing.

What not to do:

- *Don't use fancy words.* Use simple, plain English. Most people aren't impressed by big words. And you'll lose those who can't read past a certain grade level.

- *Don't use "I" like you would when talking.* Readers want to hear "you."

- *Don't let ideas flow freely and trail off.* Stay organized.

- *Don't use overly formal, bureaucratic language.* Would the person writing this really talk this way? If so, that person might be called arrogant.

- *Don't use a lot of meaningless numbers or statistics.* You wouldn't do that in a conversation, would you?

- *Don't use corporate speak.* Say what you mean in terms people understand.

- *Don't use inappropriate language.*

Here are 10 tips for writing like you talk:

1. *Use contractions like "I've," "you're" and "don't"*—they sound conversational.

2. *Use "you" and "I"* as if you were talking to a colleague.

3. *Sprinkle in phrases you use in conversation.*

4. *Start some sentences with a conjunction* such as "and," "but" or "so."

5. *Write as if you were speaking to one person,* maybe a close friend. Imagine that person is standing in front of you.

6. *Add more detail than you would when talking.* Clarify. Repeat anything a reader might have missed.

7. *Don't sidetrack.* It's common in conversation but it shouldn't occur in your writing unless you tell the reader you're going to do it.

8. *Get rid of slang and phrases only you might know.* Readers can't stop you—like they would in a conversation—to ask what you mean.

9. *Vary the length and rhythm of sentences.* Use a variety of sentence types and styles to achieve that natural feel.

10. *Use action verbs*—they convey energy.

Set the Right Tone

Your writing has an "attitude." It's your attitude toward your subject and your reader. This is your tone. Many things go into creating a tone—your writing style, the words you choose, the formality or informality of your approach, whether or not you adhere to strict grammar, the length of your sentences. Together these elements affect how the reader accepts and interprets your message so you should carefully consider tone each time you write a letter, e-mail, memo or report.

- "I hope you will have time to contact me … " may send the message that the issue is not important

- "I know that the proposal wasn't as complete as it could be … " may suggest there are other things wrong with the proposal in addition to incompleteness

What tone should you use? Once you know your purpose and who you are writing to, the tone should come naturally. If you're serious, the reader will take it seriously. If you're flippant, the reader will think the matter is of no consequence. Usually in business, it's safe to strive for a tone that is confident, professional, positive and courteous. One exception is when the purpose of the writing is to convey a negative message—such as the elimination of the company bonus system or the rejection of a vendor's contract.

- BEFORE: "I do not understand why you brought up the applicant's age in the interview."

- AFTER: "Discriminatory remarks are not tolerated in any part of the hiring process."

Not only is it important to be able to adapt your tone to different audiences, but you must also be able to adjust it to different circumstances. This means knowing when and how to be formal or informal, friendly or businesslike, approachable or more distant. Here are some of the many possibilities:

Casual:

In business, a casual tone will often be the tone of choice. It's friendly and relaxed. Readers feel like you're talking directly to them. You can achieve this tone through:

- Short sentences and paragraphs
- Frequent use of colloquial expressions like "I've been there" and "she's fed up"
- Asking questions of your reader
- Contractions such as "you're" and "I'm"
- Personal pronouns like "I," "we" and "us"
- Shorter rather than longer words
- Active rather than passive voice
- A variety of punctuation including dashes, ellipses and exclamation marks

Formal:

A formal tone is businesslike and no-nonsense. The reader feels like there is no time to waste. You can achieve this tone through:

- Longer and more complex sentences and paragraphs
- More complex and specialized vocabulary
- Formal punctuation—no dashes or exclamation marks
- Passive voice
- Avoidance of personal pronouns—and use, instead, of pronouns like "it," "one" and "they"

Persuasive:

A persuasive tone is used by advertisers to try to convince customers to buy a particular product or take a specific action. You can achieve this tone through:

- Emotionally charged words chosen to persuade your readers to feel a certain way

- Short, to-the-point sentences and paragraphs

- Logical organization of ideas

- Personal pronouns—especially "you" and "us"

To decide on the right tone, ask yourself:

- *Why am I writing this document?*

  Once you decide your purpose in writing and what you want the reader to do, the tone of your message will take shape. For example, you would use one tone if you were writing to all employees to inform them of an acquisition and another tone if you were writing to them to announce the company picnic.

- *To whom am I writing and what do I want them to understand?*

  While voice conveys *your* personality, tone reflects that of your intended audience. You will appear much more credible if your tone matches your audience's expectations. To choose the right tone, you need to know your audience and how to tailor your message to their needs.

- *How do I want to come across?*

  In business, you will usually want to sound confident, knowledgeable, polite, professional and approachable. However, the things that make up tone—stylistic choices, word choice, formality or informality, adherence or non-adherence to strict grammar, even sentence length—can be changed depending on your message.

You Try It

Imagine the statement below is the tone guideline for your company. Fill in the blanks.

The style and tone of our communications should reflect our purpose and vision. It should be _____ , _____ and _____ .

(Your company name) communicates with many audiences, each with its own needs and expectations. Remember to tailor messages for each audience, using language that is _____ , _____ , _____ and _____ while avoiding acronyms and internal jargon.

(Your company name here)'s target audiences include:

- Customers and potential customers

- _____

- _____

- _____

- _____

Grab Your Reader's Attention
With a Strong Opening

Busy readers spend maybe three seconds deciding if your document is worth reading. Many may never get past the opening of your letter or memo. So you can see why the first few words are among the most important you write. Sometimes the reason a letter or memo is written is so compelling, urgent or newsworthy it's easy to grab the reader's attention. Usually, though, you have to work at it. You have to hit your readers hard with an introduction that instantly captures their attention and makes them want to read what you've written. In addition to grabbing the reader's attention, your opening serves another purpose: It establishes a frame of reference for the reader by introducing the topic and why it should matter to the reader.

There are no right or wrong ways to start that first sentence—just as there are no right or wrong ways to start a conversation. You may think there is a "proper" way to start a business letter. But many letters get ignored because they start with the same old tired "proper" phrases:

- This is in reference to …

- Per your request …

- Enclosed please find …

- Regarding our conversation today …

- The purpose of this letter is to …

See the difference when you start with:

- You'll be glad to know …

- As you've probably guessed …

- Here's what happened …

- I'm so sorry I didn't …

- I certainly agree with you that …

- Can you help us out?

- Will you please …

- Within the next few days …

- I thought you'd be interested in this …

- Thank you for …

Writing a strong beginning doesn't start when you sit down at your computer. It starts long before. At the start of the project, you have to think about the type of document you are writing … the tone you want to convey … your reader's needs and expectations … your purpose for writing the document. When you define the one most important point you want to get across, hang on to it: This is the point you want to make early in your document.

Here are nine tips for writing a strong opening:

1. *Ask a question.* "Can you imagine our company being named Employer of the Year?"

2. *Tell a story*—one that illustrates your key point. Analogies, metaphors and similes are some of the most powerful devices available to you.

3. *Declare a fact or statistic.* "Employee theft is really costing companies a lot. *The Wall Street Journal* reports that $3 billion a year is lost when employees walk out the door with computers, supplies and other business property."

4. *Quote a famous person.* The right quote from a credible person can work wonders in holding the reader's attention those crucial first seconds.

5. *State a shocking fact.* People loved to be startled. Just make sure the fact is relevant to your message.

6. *Make a prediction* about the future and how the reader's life may be impacted.

7. *Produce a mental image.* Ask the reader to imagine this … picture this … or remember when.

8. *Create excitement* about the information to follow. "You've been chosen to represent our company at the national meeting in September!"

9. *Use "you"*—if appropriate—to involve the reader. This also will help you make it personal and establish a bond with the reader.

You Try It

Study the newsletter article below. See where the "hook" is. Is it in the opening sentence? Or further down?

High health care costs have taxpayers considering itemized deductions for medical expenses with renewed interest. As you may know, the deduction is limited to the amount of all your unreimbursed medical expenses that, when combined, exceed 7.5% of your adjusted gross income (AGI). For many individuals, surpassing the 7.5%-of-AGI floor is getting easier. Check the list below for some of the expenses you may be able to deduct.

Inspire Action With a Powerful Close

The opening of your letter is not the only place to make a big impression. The ending is just as important—if not more important. It's the last thing the reader reads. It should stay in the person's mind. It provides a sense of completeness and closure by answering the question asked in the introduction. This is not the place to introduce new ideas, arguments or evidence that might divert the reader's attention from your main purpose … or restate your main idea in overly formal and pompous language that turns readers off … or apologize for something. The purpose is to release the reader from the act of reading.

Most business writers have trouble writing a strong conclusion. They close with overused and meaningless phrases like:

- Thanking you in advance for your …

- Hoping for a prompt reply …

- I hope this answers your questions …

- Please do not hesitate to contact me …

- I hope to hear from you soon …

Here are nine tips for writing powerful closes:

1. *Keep it brief.* Say what you want to say and sign off.

2. *Resist the urge to fizzle out.* Keep the ending as strong as the rest of your document and hang on to the reader's attention.

3. *Restate your purpose* in a different way than you did in the opening.

4. *Repeat—succinctly—the key points.*

5. *Describe the next step:* "I will call the client and arrange the next meeting unless I hear from you by Friday, June 2."

6. *Leave the reader with an idea that will make them think.*

7. *Request action.* Be clear about what you want the reader to do. "Please take a moment now to call me and … "

8. *End on a positive note.* If you leave your reader with negative thoughts, you're back to square one. Add something warm and friendly.

9. *End with an emotional plea*, if appropriate.

You Try It

Echoing your opening in your closing brings your reader full-circle. Write a conclusion that follows that strategy based on the introduction below:

Introduction: *Get more for your money when you stay with an ABC Travel Co. preferred lodging partner—the best available rate for your stay and a 100% satisfaction guarantee.*

Your closing: _____

_____

_____

_____

_____

Always Give Your Message a Positive Spin

Do you consider yourself an optimist? Being an optimist isn't about being a bubblehead. It is a proven way to draw people to you. Studies show people respond more favorably to positive language. When writing, optimism is measured by how you define events. It's easy to fall into the trap of writing negatively. Many people are not even aware of doing it. Even if you don't have a negative attitude, you may be using language that gives that impression. You want people to know what you can and will do—not what you can't or won't do.

- **Negative language** states what cannot be done, comes across as blaming and focuses on negative actions and consequences. It creates a distance between you and your reader. It is sprinkled with words like:

    Fault ... Error ... Fail ... Never ... Should ... Can't ... Insist ... Overlook ...

- **Positive language** states what can be done, comes across as helpful and encouraging, offers options, alternatives and choices and focuses on positive actions and consequences. This makes it easier for readers to understand what you are saying. Positive language draws the reader in. It is sprinkled with words like:

Respect … Welcome … Thank you …. Value … Please … Satisfy … Happy … Agree

Negative	Positive
If you fail to call us by this date, we won't be able to get the shipment to you in time.	Call us by this date and we'll be happy to get the shipment to you promptly.
If you don't mail the entry form below, you won't be included in the holiday gift exchange.	Mail the entry form below now and get in on the holiday gift exchange.

And double or even triple negatives can create a real fog …

- *Double Negative:* Don't forget to not speak too loudly in the hallway.

- *Single Negative:* Don't speak too loudly in the hallway.

- *Positive:* Speak softly in the hallway.

Here are 10 tips for staying positive:

1. *Don't be a naysayer*—the person who criticizes ideas or always comes up with all the reasons why something won't work.

2. *Write from the perspective of what can be done*—not what can't.

3. *Opt for neutral words* when you can't be positive.

4. *Inject the reader's name* to warm up your writing.

5. *Don't scream* by using sarcasm or all caps.

6. *Don't use a tone that makes you sound arrogant or like a know-it-all.*

7. *Pay attention to the shades of meaning* words carry. Rather than calling it a confrontation, call it a meeting.

8. *Use antonyms to remove the negative word "not"*—rather than "he did not agree to the proposal" say "he declined the proposal."

9. *Soften your writing* by using the passive voice. Rather than "you made five mistakes in this calculation" say "five mistakes were found in this calculation."

10. *Use synonyms* to round out the edges. Rather than "it was not important" say "it was minor."

You Try It

Rewrite these negative sentences in a more positive way:

If you would only listen to me, you wouldn't have to redo the agenda.

Your rewrite: _____

_____

You claimed in your interview you had experience in accounting, but I doubt that.

Your rewrite: _____

_____

I cannot understand why in the world you would think I wanted that style of chair.

Your rewrite: _____

_____

I don't want to have to tell you that we can't refund your money.

Your rewrite: _____

_____

We regret to inform you the product you ordered is out of stock.

Your rewrite: _____

_____

We must insist you include all the paperwork with your renewal.

Your rewrite: _____

_____

Employees are not permitted to leave the premises.

Your rewrite: _____

_____

CHAPTER FIVE

Editing, Revising,
Polishing and
Perfecting Your Craft

Revision is one of the most important stages in the writing process. It's all about putting some distance between you and your writing, stepping into your reader's shoes and looking coldly and objectively at your writing. In a perfect world, you'd have access to an editor and a proofreader who could go over your work and polish it. Chances are, though, you serve as your own editor and proofreader. So you need to feel comfortable doing both functions.

Power Tip:

Remember, the most effective business documents are not written, they are re-written.

Critically Detach From Your Work

Many writers consider assessing their own writing as something they do only if they have time. But they never seem to have time. Viewing your writing objectively is hard and not a lot of fun, but it's essential. To clarify and improve your writing, you need to detach yourself, read it as if you were an unbiased outsider and check for:

- *Tone.* Imagine you are standing in the shoes of your reader. Now read your first draft. How will your reader respond to it? Is it defensive? Too formal?

- *Organization.* Are your points presented in a logical sequence? Does one paragraph flow into the next? Do your readers end up where you want them to be?

- *Purpose.* Does your first sentence or paragraph clearly state your purpose for writing?

- *Action.* Did you tell the reader what to do? Were you specific, direct, tactful?

- *Flow.* Does the document flow smoothly? Did you use good transition words to link sentences, paragraphs and ideas together?

- *Readability.* Did you use unnecessary words? Did you use passive voice when active would be stronger? Are any of the words too formal—even pretentious?

- *Grammar.* Is there subject-verb disagreement or dangling modifiers?

- *Punctuation.* Are there any serious punctuation mistakes?

- *Word usage.* Did you confuse one word for another—like continuous for continual?

- *Spelling.* Is every single word spelled correctly? If you had any doubt, did you look it up?

Here are five tips for gaining an objective viewpoint:

1. *Physically remove yourself.* Sometimes it helps to leave your office, go somewhere in your car, take a walk.

2. *Take a break.* You need to break the connection with your work and return to it with a fresh eye. Let your writing sit. It's amazing how, when you return, you'll see it with new eyes and be able to spot problem areas you didn't see before. Sometimes an hour will do it. It's ideal to let your writing sit overnight and return to it in the morning.

3. *Read it out loud.* One of the hallmarks of clear writing is writing that sounds natural—as if you were talking face-to-face with a co-worker. By hearing your writing, you'll come across repeated words, clumsy sentence construction, incomplete thoughts and other blunders you won't want to see printed.

4. *Imagine you are the reader.* When you go back and read your first draft, pretend you are the reader and you are reading it for the first time. What might be unclear? What might confuse the reader? Now that you see your writing from the perspective of your audience, you can go back and fix it.

5. *See it through someone else's eyes.* An effective way to discover how your work sounds to others is to try it out on them. Ask a colleague or someone else who most closely represents your target audience to read your draft. Ask them to tell you what they did or didn't understand. Here are some responses you will be likely to get:

   - "I have so many questions." This may mean you should explain more, elaborate and give more detail.

   - "I'm confused." More details probably won't help in this case. Explaining more clearly will. Focus on giving examples and making points that are clear.

   - "I'm bored." It's possible you've given too much detail—much more than the reader needs to know. Excessive detail is boring and can slow the reader down. It can also camouflage the big points you're trying to make.

Readers who respond in these ways are likely to become confused and frustrated and quit reading. You don't want any of these responses from readers. Instead you want them to say "Yes, I know what you're saying and I understand."

Edit Yourself to Make Good Writing *Great*

Editing is fundamental to good writing. And learning how to edit your own work is not only possible—it's necessary. Editing may be performed throughout the writing process to improve your work. It involves contextual changes that affect the meaning and presentation. It focuses on style, point of view, organization of content and audience. When editing, you should look for words and phrases that could be cut, long sentences that could be streamlined and words that could be replaced with better ones.

Your company may have its own set of rules you must follow. Or perhaps it follows *The Gregg Reference Manual, The Associated Press Stylebook*, the *SkillPath Business Communication Style Guide, The Chicago Manual of Style* or some other respected reference. Here we won't give you rules of grammar and punctuation you learned (or should have) in grade school. What you will get are tips for avoiding problems that commonly plague business writing. The goal is to prepare you to write clearly without mistakes that cause readers to question your credibility or stop reading altogether.

You need to recognize that editing requires concentration, can be painful and may take longer than the writing itself. You can't edit effectively in just one pass. It will require at least three:

1. *Edit the first time to make sure your meaning is clear.* Pretend like you're the reader. Is your message easy to understand? Simple? Will your reader have any difficulty getting your message? If you have even the slightest doubt, go back and revise.

2. *Edit the second time to polish your message.* Make sure your introduction grabs the reader's attention. Check the length of each word, sentence and paragraph—can you trim anywhere? Evaluate the order of your points—are they logical? Are paragraphs in a logical order? This is the time to replace any inappropriate language such as jargon, clichés and sexist terms.

3. *Edit the third time for accuracy.* Check the spelling, punctuation, grammar, word usage, dates, phone numbers, proper nouns and titles.

Here are 14 tips for becoming your own editor:

1. *Do a dictionary check* if you are not absolutely positive about the meaning of a word. Don't fall into the trap of thinking a word has one meaning when it has an entirely different one.

2. *Do a thesaurus check* to find words that may more accurately convey your message. But be careful—business people can easily be turned off by flowery or complicated language. So keep it simple.

3. *Do the math*—twice.

4. *Eliminate similes and metaphors that muddy your meaning.* Be direct. Say what you want to say in the simplest terms possible.

5. *Check for sentence structure.* The strongest sentences follow a subject-verb-object structure.

6. *Use your computer to check for overuse of the word "not."* Rewrite sentences the word appears in to be more positive.

7. *Eliminate unnecessary commas.* You need a comma to separate lists of things. However, don't make the mistake of using a comma when other punctuation is called for (like a semicolon) or would be stronger (like an em dash).

8. *Check for "-ing" words.* This is a sign of weak writing. Recast them.

9. *Check the order of sentences.* The most important go at the start of the paragraph.

10. *Keep related words together*—like adjectives next to the nouns they modify.

11. *Make sure each verb agrees with its subject.*

12. *Make run-on sentences into two sentences.*

13. *Make sure pronouns clearly refer to the correct nouns.*

14. *Make sure all modifying phrases and words refer clearly to the words they are to modify.*

You Try It

Do you have a document you're getting close to finishing?

Take a few minutes to complete this Editor's Checklist. It will be worth your time!

	Yes	No
The information is accurate.	☐	☐
All the information supports my purpose.	☐	☐
It is clear and easy to understand.	☐	☐
It addresses the questions a reader would ask.	☐	☐
It has an appropriate introduction and conclusion.	☐	☐
Each paragraph contains one idea.	☐	☐
The paragraphs are arranged logically.	☐	☐
All names are spelled correctly and all titles are correct.	☐	☐
I have defined any confusing terms.	☐	☐
The tone is appropriate.	☐	☐
It is free of sexist and other biased language.	☐	☐
I have eliminated unnecessary words and phrases.	☐	☐
The abbreviations are correct.	☐	☐
I explained the acronyms.	☐	☐
The document is consistent with my company's style.	☐	☐

Zero In on Spelling Trouble Spots

You may be able to get away with putting a comma in the wrong place or using "who" instead of "whom." But misspell just one word and not only will it be noticed, but your credibility will take a nose dive. Spelling problems crop up sometimes because the writer is a bad speller and doesn't know any better. But many times, spelling problems are the result of typographical errors that didn't get caught in proofreading.

Either way, misspelled words can be tough to catch. You can proof a document 10 times and not find the mistake. Then your boss zeroes right in on it. The spell-checker on your computer will catch many spelling mistakes. But just because you spell a word correctly doesn't mean it's the right word. You need a good dictionary nearby in case you're not sure. It's also a good idea to keep a list of problem words so you don't have to look the word up every time in the dictionary.

Here are some of the top spelling mistakes in business writing. A spell-checker won't catch any of them.

It's, its	This is perhaps the number one spelling error. You should routinely look at every instance to make sure you're using the word correctly. *It's* means "it is." *Its* is the possessive form of "it."
You're, your	*You're* is the contraction of "you are" and is commonly confused with the possessive *your*.
Loose, lose	*Loose* means "not bound" or "to release"; *lose* means "to suffer the loss of."
Compliment, complement	To *compliment* is to give a flattering remark; to *complement* is to complete.
Principal, principle	*Principal* can mean "leading" or "chief official of a school"; a *principle* is a general truth.
Except, accept	*Except* indicates something is left out—like an exception to the rule. *Accept* means you're receiving something, joining a group, entering into an agreement.
Affect, effect	*Affect* means "to influence or change"; *effect* means "result," "impression" or "to bring about."

There, their, they're	*There* refers to a place. *Their* indicates possession. *They're* is the contraction of the words "they are."
Were, we're, where	*Were* is a form of the verb "to be." *We're* is the contraction of "we are." *Where* is related to a place or location.
Then, than	*Then* describes a kind of time relationship. *Than* is used when comparing two or more objects.
Assure, insure, ensure	*Assure* means "to give confidence to someone"; *insure* means "to protect against loss"; *ensure* means "to make certain."

You Try It

Many misspelled words are difficult to catch—especially when you are on a deadline. Set a timer for 60 seconds, read through this list and circle the words that are spelled incorrectly. Then go back and take as much time as you need to check your choices.

accomodation	accommodation	enviroment	environment
management	managment	performance	perfomance
infomation	information	facilties	facilities
recieve	receive	excercise	exercise
independant	independent	commitee	committee
assessment	assesment	enviromental	environmental
commerical	commercial	thoughout	throughout
accomodate	accommodate	mangement	management
thier	their	resouces	resources
occured	occurred	relevent	relevant
opportunites	opportunities	administration	adminstration
activites	activities	responsibilty	responsibility
further	futher	recyling	recycling
addtion	addition	catagories	categories
committment	commitment	available	avaliable
assocation	association	governement	government
offical	official	definately	definitely
infromation	information	responsibility	responsiblity
commited	committed	responsibilites	responsibilities
realy	really		
response	reponse		
commision	commission		
throught	throughout		
goverment	government		
recieving	receiving		
sucessful	successful		
development	developement		
accross	across		

Get Grammar and Word Usage Right

In conversations at work, you can slip up grammatically and no one may notice or care. You may say "lay" when you should have said "lie" and it's not a big deal. That's not the case when writing. Make a grammatical error in an e-mail, letter or report and the mistake lives on. And you appear careless or ignorant or both. Being fastidious about grammar is all about being able to communicate effectively with your audience. When you use correct grammar, you make it easy for your readers to comprehend your message and how you want it to be interpreted. You can use your computer's grammar-checker to identify run-on sentences or overuse of the passive voice. But you're on your own for virtually all other grammar mistakes.

Here are four of the most common grammar and usage mistakes:

1. *Ambiguous pronoun reference*

   A pronoun must agree with its antecedent (the word for which the pronoun stands) in person, number and gender. The antecedent should be unmistakably clear.

   BEFORE: "John worked all week in the new building and enjoyed it very much." (Is "it" the work or the building?)

   AFTER: "John worked all week in the new building and enjoyed the change of scenery very much."

2. *Using "which" instead of "that"*

   You'll see this mistake all the time in business writing. Even the best writers are guilty of it. The rule: Use "that" to introduce essential clauses and use "which" to introduce nonessential clauses. If you're not sure, think of it this way: If you can omit the clause without damaging the sentence, use "which." If you can't, use "that." Following are examples for the correct use of both:

   "His essay, which won first prize, was about recycling."

   "The essay that won first prize was about recycling."

3. *Misused words*

    Here are some commonly misused words you need to keep in mind.

    - *Infer* means "deduce" … *imply* means "suggest"
    - *Due to* means "caused by" … not "because"
    - *Comprises* means "includes" or "consists of" … *compose* means "makes up"
    - *Adopt* means "borrow or put into practice" … *adapt* means "change or adjust (to)"
    - *Adverse* means "unfavorable" … *averse* means "opposed to"
    - *Advice* means "a suggestion" … *advise* means "make a suggestion"
    - *Between* refers to two persons or things … *among* refers to more than two
    - *Can* indicates ability … *may* indicates possibility or permission

4. *Unclear expressions*

    You want to be exact with readers. Don't leave any question or doubt about what you mean.

    - Very good response
    - Substantial savings
    - Highly recommended
    - Frequently used
    - As soon as possible

Just Say No to Punctuation Mistakes

In your business dealings, how many times does punctuation come up? Probably never—unless it's wrong. If you're like most business writers, you probably don't think much about punctuation. But you should. Misused punctuation can not only confuse your reader, but can give the impression that you're careless and haven't given your document much thought. Basically, punctuation is needed where you pause as you read. So one way to check whether you're using punctuation correctly is to read your writing out loud. If there's a break at the end of a thought, make that the end of the sentence. Don't add commas unless you're making a list or there is a natural pause in the sentence. If you don't know for sure which punctuation to use when, these simple rules will help you avoid some of the worst errors.

Here are the top punctuation mistakes to avoid:

- *Apostrophes in the wrong place*

  It's important to get apostrophes right for clarity and for professional correctness. You want to write "the employees' preferences" or "the vice president's responsibility" or "the secretary's training manual."

  If you're not sure where to put the apostrophe, reverse the phrase like this:

  - "The preferences of the … "
  - "The responsibility of the … "
  - "The training manual of the … "

  and put the apostrophe (and an additional *s* if needed) after that word.

- *Misuse of hyphens*

  Hyphens are confusing. Do you hyphenate compound words, combine the words as one word or use them as two words? If you're not sure, first go to the dictionary.

  When using a compound adjective with a noun, hyphenate when the adjective appears before a noun but not if used after it.

  Example: "The annual report contains the most up-to-date information." ("Up-to-date" is hyphenated because it comes before the noun "information.")

  Example: "The information is kept up to date." ("Up to date" comes after the noun, so it shouldn't be hyphenated.)

- *Comma splices*

  A comma splice is a comma that comes between two independent clauses that aren't joined by a conjunction such as "and" or "but." The rule: Replace the comma with a period, a semicolon or a conjunction.

  WRONG: "The woman was kind, she often fed stray cats."

  RIGHT: "The woman was kind. She often fed stray cats."

  RIGHT: "The woman was kind; she often fed stray cats."

  RIGHT: "The woman was kind, and she often fed stray cats."

- *Dangling modifiers*

  A dangling modifier is a word or phrase that modifies either no word or the wrong word in a sentence.

  BEFORE: "After walking through the production area, the improvements were still unclear."

  AFTER: "After walking through the production area, the CEO thought the improvements were still unclear."

- *Misplaced quotation marks*

  The rule: Closing quotation marks always go outside of periods and commas, even if the quoted material is not a direct quotation but is used ironically.

  BEFORE: He felt safe because he had "connections".

  AFTER: He felt safe because he had "connections."

- *Leaving out the comma after introductory elements*

  The rule: When starting a sentence with an introduction or background information, place a comma after that introductory element.

  BEFORE: "Before requesting pregnancy leave Mary completed the priority project."

  AFTER: "Before requesting pregnancy leave, Mary completed the priority project."

- *Multiple exclamation points*

  The rule: You should rarely use exclamation points in business writing. If you must, do not use more than one exclamation point.

  BEFORE: "This is unbelievable!!!"

  AFTER: "This is unbelievable!"

You Try It

The misuse of one word is causing serious problems in this Web site copy. Can you find it?

We offer over 15 years experience in providing clients with highly personalized and targeted marketing solutions. We have developed long-term relationships with many of our clients that allow us to know their business just like an inside employee—with a full understanding of their product line.

Our staff includes Jane Doe, a designer who got her first taste of layout and design while working for The Daily News back when pages were literally cut and pasted per page. For several years' she had her own shop designing and printing posters and newsletters.

If you guessed the problem word is "years" in the first and last lines, you've got a sharp eye. The apostrophe should go after "years" in the first line because it's considered possessive. It doesn't belong with "years" in the last line. An easy way to tell the difference? If you can put "of" or "worth of" after "years"/"months"/"cents"/etc., you need the apostrophe; if not, you don't.

Proofreading Made Easy

Proofreading involves reading a document to find and correct any errors. The skill of proofreading is essential, whether you are creating lots of business documents every day or just a few. Proofreading is not editing. Proofreaders catch errors in spelling, punctuation, grammar and word usage. There are systematic procedures you can follow to ensure the best results. Proofreading is usually the last stage. It involves the comparison of the writer's version and the final proof. In the case of business writing, the proof is often the copy you run from your computer.

Break proofreading down into specific steps so you don't feel overwhelmed:

- *Comparison:* This requires a word for word, character for character comparison of the final proof to the most recently edited draft. It's an important step when you are proofing numbers, columns of figures and technical data.

- *Content:* Once you have comparison proofed, proof to make sure the document makes sense and reads well. Look for sentence structure, logic, spelling, punctuation and facts. You also need to watch for consistency of style and tone.

- *Format:* This is the stage when you make sure the format is correct and consistent. The text should be justified correctly, spacing between words should be consistent and page numbers should be correct.

Types of errors to watch for when proofreading:

- Misspelled words (pay special attention to proper nouns, whose correct spelling isn't always obvious)

- Incorrect dates

- Reversed numbers

- Words or phrases typed twice in a row

- Omissions of words or parts of words

- Incorrect or missing punctuation

- Non-agreement of subject and verb

Here are 12 proofreading tips:

1. *Read your document out loud, if possible.*

2. *Proof from a hard copy*—not your computer screen.

3. *Allow some time between when you write the document and when you proof it.* You need a fresh eye to catch every typo and mistake.

4. *Use the spell-check function on your computer,* but don't depend on it to catch everything.

5. *Ask another person to double-check your document.* Make *sure* someone else reads it if it is extremely important.

6. *Read bottom to top, right to left.* This will slow you down and ensure you look at each word.

7. *Read down columns of numbers* even if they're meant to be read across.

8. *Point with your finger* and read one word at a time.

9. *Don't proof for every type of mistake at the same time.* Proof once for spelling errors, again for grammar errors and so on.

10. *Double-check little words* like "it," "a," "an" and "or."

11. *Visually scan the document.* Does it look correct? Is anything missing? Are any paragraphs too long? Are the margins correct? Is the layout style consistent?

12. *Keep a list of errors you commonly make* and proof separately for those.

You Try It

How can you do a good job of proofreading when there is little or no time? Check off each of these items and you'll be in good shape:

	Yes	No
1. I read the document out loud.	☐	☐
2. I printed a copy to proof rather than proofed from my computer screen.	☐	☐
3. I set the document aside for a while after writing it and before proofing it.	☐	☐
4. It is clear what action the reader is supposed to take.	☐	☐
5. No paragraph is too long.	☐	☐
6. There are no run-on sentences.	☐	☐
7. All words are spelled correctly.	☐	☐
8. All grammar errors have been corrected.	☐	☐

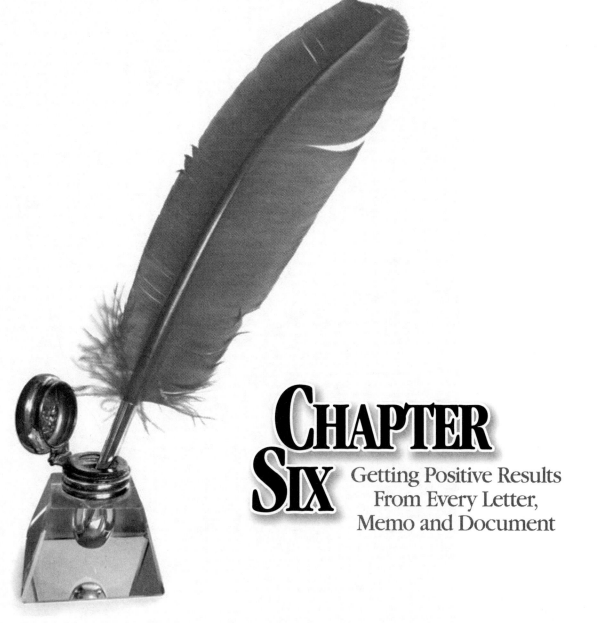

CHAPTER
SIX
Getting Positive Results
From Every Letter,
Memo and Document

Have you ever thought about how much business correspondence never gets read? E-mails, letters, memos, proposals, business plans, meeting minutes and Web pages that are too wordy, too long and too boring are being tossed daily. The writer's time is wasted and so is the reader's. That's why you should take the time to write well the key business documents you use every day.

Letters: Keep Them Brief, Straightforward and Polite

Even though you may live by e-mail, you still need to know how to write a formal letter. A letter is often the most appropriate method of communication. For example, you may write a letter to confirm an agreement made by e-mail, to discuss a legal matter, to communicate with a superior or when the communication will be seen by many other people. Because of its formal nature, a business letter is judged on small but important things like the opening and closing, conciseness and format.

Versatile and effective writers know how to write letters that are clear on several levels, regardless of what they are writing.

- The message must be clearly conveyed so that any reader can immediately understand it.

- The ideas must be presented logically and lead to one conclusion.

- The paragraphs must be in logical sequence and walk the reader through the document.

- The sentences must be direct, crisp and easily understood.

Usually, a letter includes letterhead information or return address, date, inside address, salutation, subject line (optional), body, complimentary closing, writer's name and title, reference initials, enclosure notation (if applicable), copy notation (if applicable) and P.S. (if applicable).

The Survival Store
888 N. First Street
Yourville, MO 64137-2716
(816)555-5555

May 1, 2008

Mr. John Doe
ABC Communication Co.
123 Main Street
Anytown, MO 64112

Dear Mr. Doe,

Subject: Refund for Fax Machine [this line is optional]

We are experiencing problems with the fax machine we purchased from you last week. As a result, we're returning it to you today. We are requesting our money back, per our discussion today by phone. You asked me to describe in writing the problems we're having so you can investigate it with your supplier. The key problems are:

- The feed capacity is not fast enough to meet our needs

- The design of the tray complicates paper loading

- The print quality does not meet our standards

Because of the number of problems, we are unable to meet our business needs using your product and are requesting an immediate refund.

Sincerely,

Jane Smith
Purchasing Manager

JS: ma

Enclosure

cc: Susan Jones

P.S. We appreciate your prompt attention to this matter.

Common mistakes made when writing letters:

- *Failure to define the purpose of the letter*

  If you are not clear about the purpose of your letter, your reader most certainly won't be either. Before you begin writing, ask yourself: Why am I writing this letter? What do I hope happens as a result? What is the best way to achieve this result? What information should I provide?

- *Failure to hook the reader with the first paragraph*

  The first paragraph of the letter should introduce the subject matter and either state or imply your purpose in writing. You have about three seconds to hook your reader. Don't waste time by beating around the bush.

- *Failure to tell the reader what you want to happen*

  If, by the final paragraph, your readers don't know what's expected of them, you've wasted your time and your readers'. You need to spell out your expectations in simple and plain terms.

- *Inappropriate tone*

  The tone can make or break your letter. You don't want to sound too casual, formal, clever or funny. Nor can you afford to let your feelings get the best of you. Be clear and to the point, but not blunt or offensive.

- *Addressing letters "To Whom It May Concern"*

  Why should a reader listen when you haven't taken the time to look up their correct name and title? Find out the name of the specific person you are writing to and use it. The letter will probably get to its destination faster and be more likely to get answered.

- *Addressing the reader as "Dear Sir" or "Dear Sirs"*

  If you haven't been able to determine the name of your addressee and are unsure of the gender of your reader, use a salutation like: "Dear Purchasing Manager" or "Dear Benefits Coordinator."

- *No signature*

  Even if you type your name at the end of the letter, you still need to sign in your own handwriting for that personal touch.

- *Handwriting letters*

  Handwriting a brief thank-you note might be okay. Otherwise, all business correspondence must be typewritten.

Here are eight tips for improving your letters:

1. *Use a common and accepted format.* Check current style guides for examples.

2. *Don't be vague.* State your purpose. Get to the point—most people don't have the patience to read a long-winded letter.

3. *Be courteous and professional.* Even if you are responding to a cranky customer, simply state the problem and any other relevant information. Avoid any comments that could be considered threats.

4. *Keep it short.* Try three paragraphs. The first paragraph states why you are writing. The second paragraph gives the background information and details. The third paragraph summarizes your key points and asks the reader to take action or specifies what is to happen next.

5. *Conclude by repeating what you want the reader to do*—call by a certain date, return a form, answer a question and so on.

6. *Read it before you sign it.* Make sure it makes sense and is accurate.

7. *Don't start every paragraph with "I"* … "I know" … "I believe" … "I am sure" …

8. *Check for mistakes.* Your letter must be letter-perfect before sending.

You Try It

How would you evaluate this letter? Read it and check it against the checklist that follows:

Dear Employee,

As the economy changes and consumers and businesses feel the pinch, strategies for collecting money and avoiding legal liability are becoming increasingly valuable. However, relevent statutes and rules frequently only provide a summary statement of the remedies available to the judgment creditor and the legal mechanisms for recovery.

You are invited to attend a workshop on this subject. Attend and you'll recieve practical techniques and strategies for effectively utilizing those enforcement statutes, rules and procedures available to the judgment creditor and debtor. Use our invaluable tips for successful judgment collection. The faculty will cover every aspect of collection law and procedures, including credit applications and personal gaurantees and common bankruptcy issues and solutions. You'll have the skills you need to maximize recovery even if the debtor has filed a bankruptcy petition. Space is extremely limited. If you don't let us know by Friday at 8 am if you plan to attend, you will not be allowed in.

Sincerely,

Your Human Resources Department

Checklist:

	Yes	No
Are the ideas presented in a logical order?	☐	☐
Is it well-organized?	☐	☐
Does each paragraph focus on one idea?	☐	☐
Is the message clear?	☐	☐
Does it contain active voice? Concrete nouns? Strong verbs?	☐	☐
Does it exclude fluff the reader doesn't need to know?	☐	☐
Is all the information accurate?	☐	☐
Are the grammar, spelling and punctuation proper?	☐	☐
Is the tone appropriate? Courteous? Serious?	☐	☐
Does the reader know what to do next?	☐	☐

Memos: Cut to the Chase

A memo is sent instead of a letter when the information being communicated is less important and does not leave the office. You may send a memo to inform readers of something specific—like a meeting or a change in procedure. You may also write a memo to remind others to take action, give you feedback on an issue or respond to a situation. Because they are usually sent to co-workers and colleagues, memos are less formal than business letters sent outside your organization. A memo can have a long life. Be sure yours are professional.

The format of a memo can vary from company to company. In general, most are made up of a heading such as "Interoffice Memorandum" and the lines for Date, To, From and Subject. There should be a space for a signature, followed by, if applicable, reference initials, attachment notation and courtesy copy notation.

Memo

Date: May 1, 2008
To: John Doe
From: Jane Smith
Subject: Re: Fax machine Problems

We are still experiencing problems with the fax machine we purchased from you last week. The problems are:

- The feed capacity is not fast enough to meet our needs

- The design of the tray complicates paper loading

- The print quality does not meet our standards

I feel we should check into sending this equipment back and get a replacement from another supplier. I don't feel confident your current supplier can meet our needs.

Jane

JS/ma

Attachment: Copy of invoice

cc: Susan Jones

Common mistakes when writing memos:

- *Failure to provide context*

  The employees in your organization probably receive many memos. A great many of these may be simply FYI memos. That's why the first sentence of your memo is so important. It needs to quickly tell the reader why you are writing— for example, in response to a situation or as a reminder.

- *Text-heavy*

  You probably have received memos that appear to be a solid page of text—one long paragraph. You can use lists to draw attention to specific information and present it in a visually appealing way. Lists are great for conveying steps, procedures or decisions. For example:

  To earn the Employee of the Month award, you need to meet three requirements:

  - Perfect attendance for the previous year
  - No disciplinary problems
  - Recommendations of two upper-level managers

- *Too informal*

  It's okay to use a fairly informal tone when writing memos because most will be going to those working within your company. You can refer to colleagues by their first names and use humor. But be careful—you can't afford to sound too casual. If you would be embarrassed to have your boss or the president of your company read your memo, then it needs to be rewritten.

- *Too long*

  A memo should be a short and concise document. If you have to include detailed information and your memo will be more than one page, consider using the memo to introduce the additional information and then turning the actual information into a separate report.

- *Too personal*

  Don't put anything in a memo that's too private. Once you send a memo, it becomes the property of the recipient and anyone that person chooses to share it with.

Here are nine tips for writing memos:

1. *Consider your audience.* This should include your readers' needs, background and status in the company.

2. *Keep it concise.* The shorter the better—one page or less. Use attachments for any additional information.

3. *Be specific in the subject line.* Let readers know instantly why you are writing.

4. *Get to the point.* Start by stating what the point of the memo is and what you want the reader to do.

5. *Use bullets and lists* to organize ideas and make reading easy.

6. *Be coherent.* Limit each paragraph to one idea.

7. *State the facts.* Avoid emotionally charged words.

8. *Format for readability.* While following company-specific guidelines, make your memo as reader-friendly as possible.

9. *Spend a little extra time re-checking.* A memo says something about your professionalism and credibility. Memos can be around a long time—in files and on the desks of people you never realized would see them.

You Try It

The memo below could have served as a great opportunity to motivate employees but it fell short. Do you know why?

TO: All Employees
FROM: John Smith, CEO

I am always happy when this time of year arrives. Not just because it is the holidays. But because I have the opportunity to communicate with the members of our organization. You all have provided many hours of work going toward the achievement of our goals. Your hard working efforts is appreciated. To that end, I am very pleased to tell you that we will be giving to each employee an end of the year bonus equaling 5% of your regular monthly salary. This is a one-time bonus. Unfortunately, if you don't work as hard next year, it will be discontinued. Thank you for all your hard work and wishing you a successful and happy new year.

E-mail: Sound Business Writing Principles Apply Here Too

E-mail is probably the primary way you do business these days. It's a serious form of business communication that many take lightly but shouldn't. As the least formal type of business communication, it can't be used for everything. You can use e-mail for informal matters such as reminders and questions or when it's preferred by the recipient. Unfortunately, too many e-mails are written quickly, without much thought and without checking for spelling, punctuation, grammar and other errors. You must apply sound business writing principles to e-mail too.

To: "John Doe" (John.Doe@ABC.com)
Subject: Fax Machine Problems
Date: Mon., May 1, 2008

John:

We are still having problems with the fax machine we purchased from your supplier.

- The feed capacity is not fast enough to meet our needs.

- The design of the tray complicates paper loading.

- The print quality does not meet our standards.

I feel we should check into sending this machine back to you and get a new one from a different supplier. I don't feel confident about the equipment coming from this supplier.

Attached is our original purchase contract.

Thanks,

Jane

Common mistakes when writing e-mails:

- *Sending nasty e-mails.* Even if you think you are anonymous because you use a separate e-mail address, your e-mail can still be traced back to you. Don't even think about sending off-color comments, catty remarks or off-the-cuff statements about anyone to anyone.

- *Clicking "send" too fast.* You have to check every e-mail before you send it for misspelled words, missing words and other careless errors.

- *Omitting the subject line.* The subject line is essential if you want people to open your e-mail instead of delete it. If this line is empty it looks like your e-mail is not important.

- *Writing a meaningless subject line.* Never write "hello" or "follow-up" or other generic subject lines. Your subject line should be relevant to your message and "hook" the reader.

- *Failing to personalize your e-mail.* Use the person's name in a salutation to add that personal touch—for example, "Dear Mary" or simply "Mary."

- *Inappropriate tone.* Think twice about the tone of your e-mail before you send it. Because your reader cannot hear your voice or see your facial expressions, your message can be interpreted the wrong way. Choose your words carefully.

- *Making jokes.* For the same reasons as just mentioned, it is easy for a joke to be misconstrued. Don't risk it.

- *Writing too much.* E-mail is supposed to be short. Include only a few paragraphs at most. Keep it brief and scannable.

- *Omitting your contact information at the end.* Contact information makes it easier for your reader to contact you later, if necessary. Get into the habit of using a signature block with all your pertinent information.

- *Failure to edit and proof before sending.* Because e-mail is a casual form of communication, many people think the rules of professional business writing don't apply. But they do. So always check your spelling, grammar, punctuation— everything—before you send your message.

Here are nine tips for writing professional e-mail:

1. *Decide on the main points* you want to make *before* writing the e-mail.

2. *Create a subject line that will instantly let readers know this message is relevant and important to read.*

3. *Use bullets for your key points.* Attach a file with the complete details. Tell readers they can refer to it for more information.

4. *Follow the rules of clear business writing:* Use active voice, keep sentences and paragraphs short, stick with one- and two-syllable words, avoid jargon and acronyms readers don't understand, use boldface (sparingly) for emphasis and tell readers what you want them to do.

5. *Watch your tone*—avoid humor and sarcasm because your message may be misunderstood.

6. *Be positive and polite.* Say please and thank you.

7. *Never use e-mail to deliver bad news.*

8. *Watch your legal Ps and Qs*—don't say anything that could come back to haunt you.

9. *Don't use emoticons or chat room shorthand.*

Be careful if you're angry or emotional

Never dash off an e-mail or memo just to get something off your chest. Don't put words in CAPITAL LETTERS for emphasis. Or threaten. Or berate. A CEO of a major health care software development company did just that. The biting e-mail he wrote was meant for about 400 employees, but was leaked onto the Internet and read around the world. Business analysts say he violated two cardinal rules of modern management:

1. Never hold large-scale discussions by e-mail.

2. Never use company e-mail to convey sensitive or controversial information to more than a few trusted employees.

At the end of the week, the company's stock fell. While analysts agree other factors probably contributed to the drop, they agree the e-mail had something to do with it. Take a look—we removed only the names and company-specific references:

From: CEO
To: ALL MANAGERS
Subject: MANAGEMENT DIRECTIVE: Week #10-01: Fix it or changes will be made
Importance: High

To the XX-based managers:

I have gone over the top. I have been making this point for over one year.

We are getting less than 40 hours of work from a large number of our XX-based EMPLOYEES. The parking lot is sparsely used at 8AM; likewise at 5PM. As managers -- you either do not know what your EMPLOYEES are doing; or YOU do not CARE. You have created expectations on the work effort which allowed this to happen inside XXXX, creating a very unhealthy environment. In either case, you have a problem and you will fix it or I will replace you. NEVER in my career have I allowed a team which worked for me to think they had a 40 hour job. I have allowed YOU to create a culture which is permitting this. NO LONGER.

At the end of next week, I am plan to implement the following:

1. Closing of Associate Center to EMPLOYEES from 7:30AM to 6:30PM.

2. Implementing a hiring freeze for all XX-based positions. It will require Cabinet approval to hire someone into a XX-based team. I chair our Cabinet.

3. Implementing a time clock system, requiring EMPLOYEES to 'punch in' and 'punch out' to work. Any unapproved absences will be charged to the EMPLOYEES vacation.

4. We passed a Stock Purchase Program, allowing for the EMPLOYEE to purchase XXXX stock at a 15% discount, at Friday's BOD meeting. Hell will freeze over before this CEO implements ANOTHER EMPLOYEE benefit in this Culture.

5. Implement a 5% reduction of staff in XX.

6. I am tabling the promotions until I am convinced that the ones being promoted are the solution, not the problem. If you are the problem, pack you bags.

I think this parental type action SUCKS. However, what you are doing, as managers, with this company makes me SICK. It makes me sick to have to write this directive.

I know I am painting with a broad brush and the majority of the XX- based associates are hard working, committed to XXXX success and committed to transforming health care. I know the parking lot is not a great measurement for 'effort'. I know that 'results' is what counts, not 'effort'. But I am through with the debate. We have a big vision. It will require a big effort. Too many in XX are not making the effort.

I want to hear from you. If you think I am wrong with any of this, please state your case. If you have some ideas on how to fix this problem, let me hear those. I am very curious how you think we got here. If you know team members who are the problem, let me know. Please include (copy) XXXXX in all of your replies.

I STRONGLY suggest that you call some 7AM, 6PM and Saturday AM team meetings with the EMPLOYEES who work directly for you. Discuss this serious issue with your team. I suggest that you call your first meeting -- tonight. Something is going to change.

I am giving you two weeks to fix this. My measurement will be the parking lot: it should be substantially full at 7:30 AM and 6:30 PM. The pizza man should show up at 7:30 PM to feed the starving teams working late. The lot should be half full on Saturday mornings. We have a lot of work to do. If you do not have enough to keep your teams busy, let me know immediately.

Folks this is a management problem, not an EMPLOYEE problem. Congratulations, you are management. You have the responsibility for our EMPLOYEES. I will hold you accountable. You have allowed this to get to this state. You have two weeks. Tick, tock.

/signed/

Chairman & Chief Executive Officer
XXXX Corporation

Reports: Stick to the Facts and Speed Up Decision Making

If your professional success is linked to the reports you write, you need to make sure those reports get read, understood and acted upon. Following a sound approach to writing reports will help you use your time effectively and produce a document that supports—rather than slows down—decision-making. The typical audience for business reports is upper level managers with little or no technical knowledge. Without a doubt, conveying your ideas clearly and persuasively will help you gain recognition and influence among these higher-ups as well as throughout your organization.

Why will your reader be reading the report? This is one of the most valuable questions to ask. There may be a wide range of answers. Readers may be seeking:

- A complete introduction to the issue

- Information they can use to persuade a boss or client to take some action

- Information they can use to evaluate their own idea—or someone else's

- A review of other expert opinions

- A brief overview to avoid embarrassment when the issue is discussed later

The truth about reports is that writing them can involve a lot of time, and few people will read the entire report from start to finish. It's important that you write and format the report so others can get the information you want them to get without spending a lot of time reading. Most readers will read the summary, conclusions and recommendations. They also want to know that, should they need to go back into the report for more details, they'll be able to find those details quickly and easily.

A smart strategy is to stick with a standard report-writing format. Specific information needs to be in specific places.

A report usually consists of these sections:

- *The title section.* In a short report, this may be just the front cover, which should include the author's name and the date. In a long report, it may include a table of contents.

- *The summary.* This is probably the section most often read, especially by business executives. It is where you explain what you're planning to do and how you're planning to do it. It includes a summary of the main points, conclusions and recommendations within the report. It is short, concise and free from jargon and confusing technical language so anyone can understand it.

- *The terms of reference.* This introductory part of the report says who the report is for, what the report is about and when the report needs to be presented.

- *The introduction.* This is where the issue is introduced, the scope of the research or investigation is described, background is given and the reader is told why the issue matters. The introduction will also explain what's to come in the report and how the reader can expect the information to be presented.

- *The body.* This may consist of different sections and subsections. It presents all the relevant facts and what the writer has learned about the issue. The points are presented logically and in order of importance.

- *The conclusion.* This brings all the information together and presents the logical conclusions of the investigation of the issue. The interpretation of the results should be translated into plain English for those with little or no technical knowledge. Possibly, many people will read this section. Be careful with the findings and interpretations of the results you present. Conclusions and future studies may be based on this section.

- *The recommendations.* These are the writer's suggestions for what action should be taken.

- *The appendices.* These might be read only by specialists or experts. This is where to present additional, possibly more detailed or technical, information referred to in the report, such as tables and graphs.

Common mistakes when writing reports:

- *Long, complex sentences.* Try breaking up complex sentences into simple ones.

- *Opinions.* Reports should stick with the facts, based on the evidence.

- *Informal language.* The language must be formal—no slang.

- *First person language—using "I" or "me."* Always use third person language.

- *Not being clear on which type of report you're supposed to be writing.* Does your company or client want a business plan, business proposal, strategic plan, strategic business plan, marketing plan, financial plan—or some other type of report? Know exactly what type of final report is expected from the outset.

- *Not including headings and subheadings.* The main parts of your report should have headings. Important parts inside these main areas should carry subheadings.

- *Writing the table of contents last instead of first.* The table of contents is one of the most important sections of the report. It is a step-by-step plan for writing the rest of the report. The time and thought you put into it in advance will definitely pay off.

- *Writing the report separately from the table of contents.* The table of contents is a skeleton of your report, complete with headings and subheadings. If you start at the beginning of the table of contents and work your way through to the end—filling in the blanks—the actual writing process will be much easier.

Here are 10 tips for writing effective reports:

1. *Make writing a group activity.* Encourage colleagues to give their input.

2. *Be concise.* Short reports are more likely to be read than long ones.

3. *Use simple, straightforward language.* Don't try to impress people with flowery language or esoteric vocabulary.

4. *Include only the information that is necessary.*

5. *Don't preach or lecture.* Just present the facts.

6. *Don't use the passive voice.* It screams "bureaucracy."

7. *Use interesting illustrations to make your point—in color, if possible.*

8. *Make sure the Executive Summary can stand alone and makes sense to a non-technical audience.*

9. *Use tables and graphs to demonstrate results.*

10. *Don't introduce any new information in the conclusion.* Stress the importance of your research instead.

You Try It

Critically review a report you wrote or one you received from someone else.

List the strengths of the report. For example: The Executive Summary was strong and concise.

1. _____

2. _____

3. _____

Now list some of the weaknesses you see:

1. _____

2. _____

3. _____

When you sit down to write a report, ask yourself: How can I build on these strengths and eliminate these weaknesses?

Proposals: Inform, Persuade and Sell

Have you ever spent hours writing a proposal only to have a competitor win the business? If you want to write polished and professional proposals that land clients and business, there's one big thing to remember: *The proposal should be about your reader and not about you.*

A well-written proposal is a powerful sales tool. It should answer all the reader's questions and persuade the reader to do something—to buy your product, give you support, give you permission, request your service. There are many different types of proposals, but all should answer some basic questions: What is the problem being addressed? Why is the problem important? What will you do to address the problem? How will you bring the reader closer to the overall solution?

A proposal usually consists of these parts:

- *Introduction.* This section should be short and to the point. Tell the reader that the document to follow is a proposal. Also refer to your previous contact with the reader—perhaps you just talked on the phone or met at a trade show. Or refer to your source of information about the project—maybe your boss asked you to put something together. Include a short sentence that will motivate the reader to continue to read. Provide a summary of what is to follow.

- *Background.* This section is where you explain why there is a need for your product or service—what problem, opportunity or situation has occurred that you can help with. For example, a direct mail company may need to comply with new postal regulations regarding how third class mail is sorted. Your product and service will make compliance easier and more cost-effective. It's possible the reader doesn't even know there's a problem that needs to be addressed. This is your opportunity to expand their awareness.

- *Description of your solution.* Tell the reader what your solution to the problem is—what's involved, how it would work and the results. Be sure to describe the benefits of your solution—how your solution will help the reader save money, save time, achieve compliance, take advantage of an opportunity or eliminate a problem.

- *Description of how you'll do the work.* To gain their confidence, show the reader you have a sound plan. Focus on the technical aspects of the solution. In the case of the mailing solution, describe your equipment, how fast it runs, what the company would need to provide to you in terms of their mailing lists and materials and so on.

- *Schedule.* Give the projected completion date, key milestones and a timeline if the project is long-term. Tell the reader how long each phase of the project will take—for example, how much time you need to process the mailing list, sort, mail and so on.

- *Qualifications.* Briefly summarize your or your organization's qualifications to do the proposed work. Include how long you've been in business, your work experience, similar projects you've completed, references and any certifications or training experiences that set you apart from others.

- *Costs, resources required.* You may need to give information such as your hourly rates or rates by project, how many hours it will take and the costs of equipment and supplies. Add all the costs to come up with the total cost of the project. Do not discuss costs until now—after you've sold the reader on your qualifications and the benefits you can provide.

- *Conclusions.* Conclude by reviewing the benefits of your product or service, and encourage the reader to contact you promptly to work out the details.

Common mistakes when writing proposals:

- *Confusing structure.* Readers need to be led through the proposal. They want to know what's coming and where they've been. Each section must be presented in a logical order. For example, don't tell the reader the solution until you've told them what the problem is.

- *Text-heavy.* People are busy and most won't take the time to read your entire proposal—at least in one sitting. You can use a variety of techniques to break up the text—such as white space, headings, subheadings, marginal notes, introductions to sections, prefaces, summaries and appendices with charts and diagrams.

- *Choppy transitions.* When you're shifting perspectives between sections, paragraphs and sentences, don't lose the reader. Refer to earlier discussions and repeat key words and phrases to allow for smooth transitions.

- *Too much jargon.* Some of your readers may understand technical jargon, but others may not. Make an effort to discuss technical concepts in plain, everyday English.

- *Failure to identify exactly what your solution is.* Tell the reader in direct language exactly what you are proposing to do—for example, whether you'll perform all the steps in their mailing operation or handle only the sorting part.

Here are five tips for writing proposals:

1. *Start early.* You may need to depend on other people for information. You don't want to be scrambling at the last minute to throw something together.

2. *Follow the instructions.* Certain organizations—especially the government—have specific requirements and formats. If you don't follow them, your proposal won't be accepted.

3. *Establish your credibility.* Describe your experience. Include resumes of staff if appropriate. Your reader's impression of you as a qualified organization depends not only on what you say you can do but who you are.

4. *Don't be sloppy.* Demonstrate your attention to detail. Make sure everything is perfectly accurate—your spelling, grammar, punctuation and calculations. The skill with which you prepare your proposal reflects your standards.

5. *Use the buyer's words and phrases.* This will help you connect faster and show you've bothered to do your homework.

You Try It

Pull out a proposal you received that did not win your business. Why didn't you give the company your business?

- Was the proposal unclear—maybe even incoherent?

- Was the information that was presented inconsistent with what was presented on the company's Web site, brochure, data sheet?

- Was important information left out—like the implementation plan, post-sale support, payment terms?

- Other reason(s) _____

Press Releases: Make a Busy Editor's Job Easier

If you think you'll never write press releases, you may be thinking about skipping this section. But don't. The press release is a basic tool for communicating with the media. If well-written, it can increase your sales, position your company before millions of people and enhance the image of your business or products. So it's vital that you know what you're doing should you ever need to write one.

Press releases are sent by companies and organizations to newspapers, television and radio stations and other media. They are sent to announce news—such as the release of a new product, the naming of a new executive or some other event of interest to the public. Typical topics for a news release include announcements of new products or a strategic partnership, the receipt of an award, the publishing of a book, the release of new software or the launch of a new Web site. The big thing to remember about press releases is this: Editors and reporters are busy. They are being hassled all day by PR people. They don't care about you or your news—unless you make their job easier. So that should be your goal.

There are a variety of formats used for press releases, as evidenced by the varying examples shown in different style guides and books on writing. The following is one example, with information about each component following the sample:

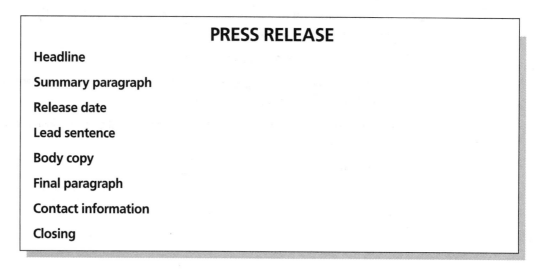

PRESS RELEASE

Headline

Summary paragraph

Release date

Lead sentence

Body copy

Final paragraph

Contact information

Closing

When using the above press release format, the following information applies:

- *Headline.* This announces the news in upper and lower case. Keep it under 80 characters.

- *Summary paragraph.* This summarizes the news and elaborates on the headline. Keep it to four sentences. Use upper and lower case and standard capitalization and punctuation.

- *Release date.* This can say: "FOR IMMEDIATE RELEASE," "FOR RELEASE (date to be released)" or "FOR RELEASE AFTER (earliest date it can be released)."

- *Lead sentence.* This sentence grabs the reader's attention in 25 words or less. It simply states the news you have to announce.

- *Body copy.* The body copy contains short sentences and paragraphs. Each paragraph is no more than four lines. The first paragraph should answer who, what, when, where, why and how questions. The rest of the news release contains information like quotes from key people and more details about the news. The entire release should contain from 300 to 800 words. The tone should be neutral and objective, not full of the hype or text that is typically found in an advertisement. Avoid directly addressing the consumer or your target audience. The use of "I," "we" and "you" outside of a direct quotation is a flag that your copy is an advertisement rather than a news release.

- *Final paragraph.* This paragraph contains the least newsworthy material. You can restate and summarize the key points. For example:

  For more information on the news that is the subject of this release, contact Jane Doe at or visit www.abccompany.com.

- *Contact information.* Include a short boilerplate background of your company before you list the contact person's name and phone number.

  About ABC Company:

  Contact: Jane Doe, Director of Public Relations

  ABC Company

  777-777-7777

  http://www.abccompany.com

- Closing. Type ### to indicate the end of the press release.

Common mistakes when writing press releases:

- *Not sticking to the facts.* Tell the truth. Do not exaggerate. If your story sounds too good to be true, editors may not believe you. Journalists do not want to get promotional copy. Focus on the news and the content.

- *Wordiness.* Be concise. Keep it to one page. Avoid adjectives, fluffy language, passive voice, jargon and hype. Make every word count.

- *Using all caps.* Don't do this. It will be ignored by journalists. Use mixed case.

- *Failure to get written permission* before including quotes from employees or anyone else affiliated with your company.

- *Not ending the release with a summary statement.* This boilerplate statement should describe who your company is, your products and services and a brief history. Keep it short.

- *Grammar and spelling errors.* Even one mistake can damage your credibility and get your release tossed.

- *Wrong formatting.* News releases are usually double spaced and limited to one page.

- *Using first person.* Write in the third person.

- *Contact information hard to find.* Put your name, address, phone and e-mail in a prominent place so editors/reporters won't have to search for it.

Here are five tips for writing press releases:

1. *Give editors what they want—news.* Don't send a press release unless the news is timely, is of interest locally, is noteworthy and has a human interest angle. Ask yourself: Will someone else find this story interesting? Why should anyone care?

2. *Pick an angle.* Make sure your story has a good news "hook." Focus on the part of your story that makes it truly unique and newsworthy.

3. *Give it to them in the format they want.* Editors and reporters are busy. They must be able to skim the first paragraph and get the information they need, so all the essential information—the who, what, when, where, why and how—must be in your first paragraph.

4. *Send it to the right person.* Too many press releases are sent to the wrong editor in the wrong department. Consequently, they are ignored. You need to know which stories are of interest to which media and target your audience accordingly.

5. *Get your release there before the editor/reporter's deadline* but not too far in advance. Press releases are typically distributed shortly before an event—usually the day before.

You Try It

Pull out a press release you recently sent or received. Ask a colleague to read it. Give them five seconds. Then ask what the release is about.

If your colleague can't give you a clear answer, the lead of the release didn't do its job and needs work.

CHAPTER SEVEN

Persuading Readers
to See It Your Way

Even if you're not in marketing or sales, you have an everyday need to sell your ideas, point of view or recommendations—and to persuade others to act upon them. Everything you write in business—from meeting agendas to budget requests to performance appraisals—has the same purpose: To elicit a response. You want someone to do something—attend your meeting, approve your budget request, change their performance.

This section will focus on the art of persuasive writing and how to successfully convince others to agree with you. You'll learn how persuasive writing is quite different from writing to inform or educate. You'll also learn how important it is to win the trust of your audience, tell them "what's in it for them," appeal to their emotions and make their decision—whatever it is—easy to make.

Build Believability With a Time-honored Persuasion Formula

You want your prospect to read your copy, believe your claims and buy. If there is any doubt in your prospect's mind, he or she won't buy, no matter how good the "deal." You can build believability into your writing by following the timeless **AIDA** formula, an extremely powerful way to get readers to act. Follow each of these steps in the correct sequence and you can feel confident you are writing a winner.

The AIDA formula is simple and time-tested:

- **A**ttention
- **I**nterest
- **D**esire
- **A**ct

Get the reader's ATTENTION

You must make sure you have your readers' attention and they're listening to you before you can sell them on your idea. You do this with a dramatic headline. A good headline draws readers in, gives them an idea of what's ahead and hints at the ways they will benefit if they read on.

- Save $10 on your favorite items

- FREE book

- Buy One, Get One Free

- Tremendous changes are facing our industry in coming months

- Are you in the career you love?

Stimulate INTEREST

You can accomplish this by showing your customers that they need your product, service or idea. For example, if you're selling your rental car company's frequent buyer program, you can tell your customers they will never again have to wait in line at the car rental desk if they become members.

Create DESIRE

You have made customers aware of their need. Now remove resistance and create desire—this is what really makes people buy into what you're selling. It's here that you provide information that expands on your promise: If readers say yes, they'll get the things they're looking for. Show them how they'll save time, advance their careers, be more persuasive, speak with more confidence in public. Whatever the key benefit is, create a visual of it in your reader's mind.

Tell your audience how to ACT

Many writers get the first three elements correct but fail to urge people to buy. Be specific about the steps they need to take to achieve these benefits. Tell them how easy it is to call today, return the enclosed card or order on-line. People won't take action unless you persuade them to do so. Compel them to act by creating a sense of urgency. Offer a bonus or special price if they respond by a certain deadline.

- This offer is only available through March 1

- Supplies are limited. Don't be disappointed. Order now!

And don't forget to back up your argument with proof:

- Inject facts and research findings to support your claims.

- Use case histories, testimonials, graphs and test results to illustrate your points.

- Cite any awards or third-party reviews the product or service has received.

- Include testimonials of satisfied customers. Stating their full names and addresses will add to your credibility.

- Use comparisons to make numbers interesting and relevant to the reader's life.

 You Try It

Persuasive Writing: Self-assessment

Factor	To what extent do I do this?	How important is it to my success?
Gain attention quickly		
Stimulate need		
Create desire		
Urge action		

This brief assessment will give you a good idea of what you do, how often you do it and how to increase your success.

Draw Readers In With Exciting Words

Words are powerful tools for expressing our thoughts to others. As a business writer, you also need to recognize the psychological and emotional impact of words. Certain highly persuasive words are like magic. By using them, you can convince your reader to take whatever action you want—call, go on-line, mail in a form. Such words can be extremely effective in motivating people to act, so use them as frequently as you can.

What kinds of words cause excitement? Think about your own work environment. Did a memo cause people in your office to sit up and take notice? Did an ad running in the local newspaper have an unexpectedly great response? Spend some time evaluating why. Take a look at the words used. Chances are, they were compelling.

Action verbs: Discover, Explore, Drive, Advance, Do, Imagine, Succeed, Gain, Prosper, Guarantee

Descriptive adjectives: Powerful, Bold, Exciting, Compelling, Proven, Secret, Free, Easy, Fast, Limited, Important

Intriguing starters: Are you still … ? Are you curious about … ? Did you know that … ? Did you ever ask yourself … ? Do you need … ? Don't you wish … ?

Exciting nouns: Breakthrough, Bonus, Testimonial, Discount, Expert, Safety, Love, Results

Intriguing transition phrases: But it gets better … , You see … , Think about it … , The truth is … , However … , First … , Frankly … , But that's not all … , Best of all …

Power Tip:

The most powerful word in the English language is "you."

You Try It

Change these ordinary words into power words. For example:
Powerful … Invincible

Ordinary word	Power word
Attractive	
Confident	
Determined	
Fine	
Intense	
Motivated	
Interesting	
Strong	

Answer the Big Question: What's In It for Me?

Writers can get so caught up in talking about *their* company, products and services that they lose sight of one major rule in writing copy that sells: Tell the audience what's in it for *them*. Why should they bother to read your letter and buy your product? Your prospect wants to know: Will it make me smarter or richer? Will it save me money or time? Help me get ahead at work? Make people like me? Give me more control? Make me feel good when I use it or buy it?

Successful promotional writers highlight the features of their product or service and then link them to benefits for their target audience:

- A *feature* is a characteristic of your product—such as its size, color and weight

- A *benefit* is what your product does *for your reader*—how it saves time, improves their status, saves money or makes them feel secure

Power Tip:

Each time you state a feature, follow it up with a benefit.

Imagine you're writing to a friend or colleague—someone you know well. If you were speaking face-to-face with this person, what would you say to convince him or her to take action? You'd talk about the features of the product—how big it is, its color, what material it's made of. But more important, you would tell about the benefits—how the product will improve your friend's life. For example, the new hybrid cars get more miles to the gallon than a traditional car. But the benefit of such a car is that your friend will spend less money on gas and have more money left over for other things. If your friend is ecologically concerned, another benefit is that this car is better for the environment. You can think of benefits as hot buttons that play into your friend's desires and wants. Figure out which ones to push and your friend will find it easy to make a buying decision.

Even a simple request gets a better response when a reader-benefit plug accompanies it:

BEFORE: "Return the card so we can update our mailing list."

AFTER: "So that health insurance premium notices, new benefit information and other messages of importance may reach you promptly, please complete and return the other half of this card."

Here are seven tips for conveying "What's In It for Me?"

1. *Apply the "So what?" test.* If the reader thinks "So what?" when reading about an aspect of your product, then that is a *feature.* Your answer to their "So what?" is a *benefit.*

2. *Don't make the customer do all the work.* Make the connection between features and benefits for them.

3. *Find out all you can about your customer.* When you put together the facts, it's easier to figure out what motivates them.

4. *Put yourself in the shoes of the buyer.* Approach your product or service like it was brand new. Then ask yourself: Why would I buy it?

5. *Think in terms of results.* Ask: What results do I get from the GPS system? electric toothbrush? whatever the product is?

6. *Write a list of 5 – 10 benefits before you even start writing.* Then think about the number one benefit and zero in on it.

7. *Don't close the sale by pitching the feature.* Pitch the benefit.

You Try It

Change the following sentences so that they emphasize the benefit to the reader:

1. *To help us cut down on overtime costs, we ask you to submit your print order 10 days in advance of the due date.*

   _____

   _____

2. *We do not send customers copies of invoices because of postage concerns. You have your canceled checks anyway.*

   _____

   _____

3. *Our brochure is designed to help its readers get the most out their company benefits package.*

   _____

   _____

4. *We allow a 2% discount for cash payments.*

   _____

   _____

5. *Since we have our own obligations to meet, we must ask you to immediately take care of your past-due balance.*

   _____

   _____

Gain Psychological Leverage

Chances are pretty good that you're not a psychologist. However, to be a persuasive writer, you must become a student of human behavior and what makes people tick. It is precisely this knowledge you use when you grab, intrigue and involve the reader by the use of psychological appeals. Using the right psychological appeal can take your writing to the next level.

People make decisions based on emotions—not just facts. A psychological appeal doesn't aim at your intellect. It aims at your subconscious mind and emotions. It doesn't have to make sense to be effective. And often it doesn't. Think of the last nightmare you had. It was all in your mind, yet you woke up shaking and breathing hard. That's because your mind controls your body. You need to arouse an emotion—like fear, pride or anger. To push these emotional hot buttons, you need to know who your audience is and what their wants, needs and desires are.

What motivates people? The truth is, wants and needs don't change much. Back in 1923, Daniel Stard published in *Principles of Advertising* a list of motivations uncovered by a study. Some of them include:

Sex …	Ambition …	Pleasure …
Approval of others …	Safety …	Curiosity …
Control …	Love of kids …	Love of parents …
Possessions …	Competition …	

Here are proven psychological appeals you may want to try:

- *Repetition.* Repetition is a common method of persuasion. The more you repeat the strengths of your product or service, the more familiar to your reader that product or service becomes. And familiarity leads to liking. When you see an ad on TV over and over for a product and then you see the product in the grocery store, you're more likely to buy it. Advertisers know this principle well. You can repeat a short phrase, a promotional message or a persistent request. Just be aware of how much repetition is too much. To be safe, make your point in different ways—directly, then by using an example, telling a story and quoting a famous person. And of course, repeat it once again in your conclusion.

- *Reasons why.* Psychological studies show that people are more likely to comply with a request if you give them a reason why. That's why, in direct mail especially, you commonly see sections of copy under a heading like "10 Reasons Why You Should Attend." You don't like to do what you're told or asked unless you're given a reasonable explanation, do you? Neither do your readers. Rather than just tell readers to "do it," give them reasons why.

- *The bandwagon effect.* This strategy is based on the belief that people often do or believe things because other people do. The need to be accepted by a group is one of the most powerful psychological forces in our lives. You can create the bandwagon effect through the use of testimonials and outside referrals and by aligning your product with an expert or celebrity.

- *Comparisons.* Using comparisons is a technique used by all the sales masters. If a customer has a concern about your product or service, you can ease their fear by using a metaphor, simile or analogy. For example, compare the cost of your technology conference to the cost of hiring a consultant to come in and advise your senior managers.

- *Empathy.* "I can relate to that." Empathy is one of the most valuable traits a persuasive writer can have. When you can put yourself in your customer's shoes, identify with their problems and feel their pain, magic happens. There are different ways to show empathy. Share an experience you had that is similar to the customer's. Use phrases like "Has this ever happened to you?" and "We've all been there." Above all, listen to customers by giving them a way to respond and contact you.

- *Predictions of the future.* People are uncertain about the future. If you tell readers what might happen (or not happen) in the future if they don't buy your product, you are in an extremely persuasive position. For example: "One year from today, you will be sitting in the corner office instead of the cubicle you're in now." But be ready to back up your claims with experience, background or credentials.

Here are six tips for using psychological appeals:

1. *Test different writing approaches* and see what works.

2. *If you can't do an extensive or formal test, talk to 10 customers.* See if you can find out what makes them tick.

3. *Remember that you are writing to human beings.* Keep in mind that they all have insecurities, needs and desires.

4. *Don't sound "corporate."* Take time to consider your readers' psychology, learn what's on their mind and decide how best to use an emotional appeal.

5. *Don't tell someone to do something.* Get them to *want* to do it.

6. *Write from the reader's viewpoint—not yours.* They are thinking about themselves, not you.

You Try It

On a scale of 1 – 5 (5 is highest), how would you rate your comfort in using these psychological appeals:

Repetition	1	2	3	4	5
Reasons why	1	2	3	4	5
Bandwagon effect	1	2	3	4	5
Comparisons	1	2	3	4	5
Empathy	1	2	3	4	5
Predictions of the future	1	2	3	4	5

Work on strengthening yourself in each of these appeals and you'll be well on your way to becoming a highly persuasive writer.

Maximize the Power of "You"

Have you ever been on the phone with someone who talked only about herself or himself? Did you feel trapped? Annoyed? Mad? You probably didn't think that person cared much about you. Nor would you seek that person out for another conversation. The same holds true for your writing. Are you writing only about all the great features of your product and all the nifty things it can do? Or are you writing about your customer—what their problems are and how your product can solve them? To your reader, "you" is the sweetest word in the universe.

Present your product from the customer's point of view. Get on your reader's wavelength. You'll find when you start writing from a "you" viewpoint, this becomes easier.

Your readers are much more concerned about themselves than about you or your company. They are more likely to read and respond to your message when they see their name and the pronoun "you" rather than "I," "we" or "us."

Of course you have to write about your company and product, but as much as possible, concentrate on your readers and how you can get them involved in your message. Help them understand it and make sure they remember it. It's easy to develop tunnel vision. You spend your days in your organization, talking about your products in your specialized "corporate speak" or "marketing speak" or "industry speak." But the language of persuasive writing is customer-focused. It's "you" instead of "we." It's about your customers and their needs—not your company and your products. Your writing needs to have a voice. And it needs to sound like your customer's. Your customers like to hear about themselves, their situations and, only as it relates to them, your product or service.

Before	After
"I want to congratulate you on your achievement."	"Congratulations on your achievement."
"We will ship the product soon."	"You should receive the product you ordered by Thursday."
"We give every employee a personal day each month."	"You earn a personal day each month."
"I think this is interesting … "	"You will find this interesting … "
"We've been in business 25 years and … "	"You know you can count on us, because we've been in business 25 years … "

Here are seven tips for gaining a "you" perspective:

1. *Begin the first paragraph with "you" or "your."* And keep using "you" throughout to make your copy personal—like you're talking directly to your prospect.

2. *Eliminate your ego.* You see it all the time … companies going on and on about themselves, how long WE'VE been in business, how WE operate, how WE are the best in the field. But customers just shrug this language off. They don't want to listen to you brag. They want to know: "What's in it for me?"

3. *Choose your words carefully.* The words you use and how you use them are telling your visitors where your focus is. And that focus should be on them. Talk about them, their needs, their wants and how they you can satisfy them.

4. *Put your copy to the test by asking: Who cares?* Your customer should.

5. *Use the reader's name for emphasis.* In addition to the greeting, use a name in one or two other critical spots to gain attention.

6. *Discuss your products with people outside your company*—preferably potential customers. Only by learning how they see your products can you truly reach them.

7. *Personalize with a story.* Bring your information to life by weaving it into a story that ties in to your reader's life. Readers love real-life examples and practical tips based on the experiences of other people, including you.

Power Tip:

Use "you" and "your" at least five times more than "we" and "our."

You Try It

Is your focus on your customer—or you?

1. Pull out a sample of your promotional or marketing copy or copy you've written to persuade someone to do something.

2. Count how many self-focused words you find such as "I," "we" and "our."

3. Count how many times you find your organization's name.

4. Now count how many customer-focused words you find such as "you" and "your."

Surprised by the results? Now you know how to fix the problem!

The 14 Habits of the Most Persuasive Writers

The goal of persuasive writing is to convince others to agree with you. Writing to persuade can be quite different from writing to inform or educate. To write persuasively you must first win the trust of your audience, then appeal to their emotions and make the buying decision easy for them. Persuasive writing boils down to answering one simple question in the reader's mind: "What's in it for me?"

The truth is, it's surprisingly easy to persuade readers to see things your way—as long as you know the handful of habits of the best business writers:

1. *They write like they talk.* They don't use big words and stuffy language. They know if their writing sounds like advertising copy, it may be the kiss of death. They know there are many words they should never use because they set the wrong tone, and can even be offensive to readers. They avoid them with a vengeance.

2. *They never wimp-out on headlines and leads.* They know that failing to grab the reader's attention instantly is a big mistake. They realize they have a matter of seconds to capture their customer's interest, and if they don't make this window of opportunity count, they'll lose them. Their mantra: Strong headlines, strong leads, strong opening paragraphs.

3. *They speak the customer's language—not jargon or "tech-talk."* They understand industry terms but know that doesn't mean everyone will. If they must use a technical term, they explain it.

4. *They position the most important information first.* They're acutely aware that readers may not make it all the way through their copy, so they tell readers early on why they're writing, why it matters to the reader and how they'll benefit.

5. *They get to the point.* They keep their sentences and paragraphs short and sharply focused.

6. *They wouldn't think of leaving out the call to action.* They tell readers exactly what they want them to do, how they should do it and by when. And they make it easy for them to do so. They know it's okay to use the same call to action phrases and words—because they work.

7. *They know their products inside out.* Thorough product knowledge is a prerequisite for writing success. They would never try to fake it and write about a product they didn't completely understand, because their readers would know.

8. *They're masters at establishing credibility.* They come across as personal, honest, clear and persuasive. They show their audience they can be trusted and are credible. They give some information on who they are and what their background and credentials are to build credibility.

9. *They follow up each feature with a benefit.* They know the features of their product are important, but that these won't make prospects buy. That's because people buy emotionally. They buy the benefits.

10. *They get specific.* They describe, in concrete terms, details of what they are selling. They make sure readers "see" themselves engaged with their idea, service or product. If price is a concern, they state the price and emphasize the value received. They give readers ideas, suggestions and points to take away and use. They don't write in generalities. They write in specifics that apply directly to the reader's own experiences.

11. *They offer evidence to support their case.* They use facts, figures, illustrations and whatever else they have to let the reader know they're worth listening to and they know what they're talking about.

12. *They set the right tone.* They use the right level of formality to show respect for the reader.

13. *They use logic and reasoning to rationalize the decision for the customer.* They tell customers they'll save money, save time, be more popular—whatever solution addresses their emotional needs.

14. *They use the most powerful word in the English language over and over ... "you."*